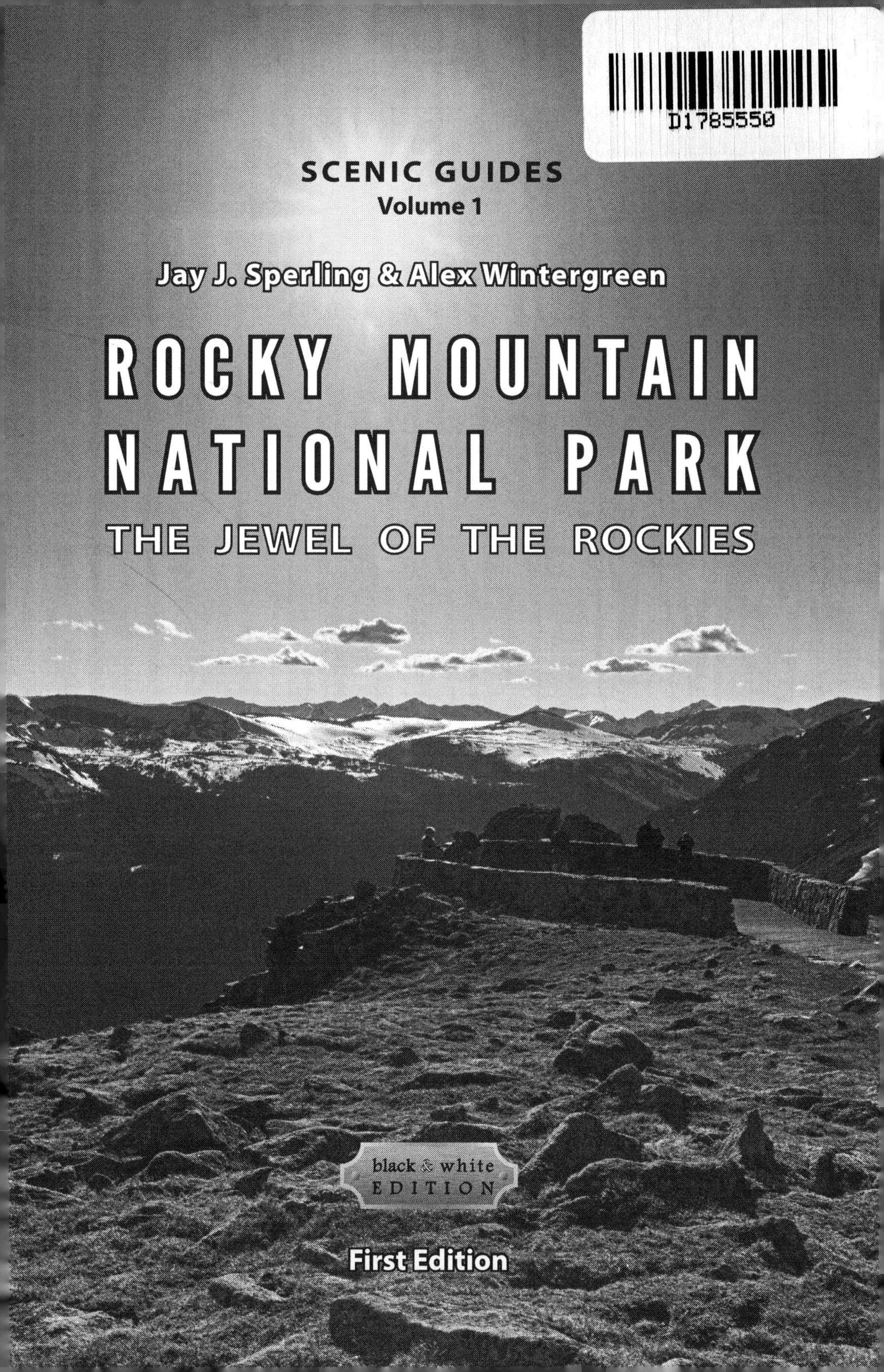

SCENIC GUIDES
Volume 1

Jay J. Sperling & Alex Wintergreen

ROCKY MOUNTAIN
NATIONAL PARK
THE JEWEL OF THE ROCKIES

black & white
EDITION

First Edition

Published by:

Rugged Feather Publishing LLC
Erie, Colorado
SAN 860-4290

All photographs by Alex Wintergreen & Jay J. Sperling
Text: Jay J. Sperling, Alex Wintergreen
Maps: All park maps are based on the official map of Rocky Mountain National Park, created by and courtesy of the National Park Service (NPS). The regional map is based on a Colorado map, created by and courtesy of the United States Geological Survey (USGS).

Front cover: Bear Lake with Longs Peak, Pagoda Mountain and Chief's Head Mountain in the back.
Title photo: Forest Canyon Overlook at sunset
Table of contents: Sunset in the Rockies
Back cover: View from the Alpine Visitor Center; young bighorn sheep ram
Painting of Moraine Park scenery on page 16: Alex Wintergreen

We value your input! Please send us feedback by e-mail: feedback@scenic-guides.com

For bulk orders please contact us: bulkorder@scenic-guides.com

First Edition

ISBN 978-1-68070-006-0

Table of Contents

INTRODUCTION

Things that Matter

As in every place where many humans visit, there are some basic rules and advices to follow in Rocky Mountain National Park so that neither people nor any other life in the park is harmed. It should be a pleasant visit — for the visitor and the visited.

1. Gear properly — The temperature change can be extreme, when you go to higher elevations. Add the wind and hide the sun behind clouds and you will find it smart to dress like an onion (in layers).

2. Drive slowly — Especially at dusk and dawn many elk and other wildlife cross the roads. Be also aware of cars that suddenly stop. They might have seen an animal to watch. Pass them safely or park and join in to watch.

3. Don't feed animals — They can get sick from improper food, they can become dependent and die because they didn't learn to care of themselves, or they can injure you because they are still wild animals.

Off-limits

4. Leave no trace — Don't twig plants, don't turn stones, don't take anything out of the park and leave everything exactly as it is.

5. Respect wildlife — Do not approach wildlife. If wildlife changes its behavior, you are too close. Step back and watch from a greater distance.

6. Campfires — Fires are only allowed on campgrounds and designated fire pits in picnic areas. Collecting wood is prohibited, hence bring your own firewood.

7. Dogs are not allowed on the trails — Dogs are only allowed on streets, in parking areas and on campgrounds.

Fenced area

8. It is allowed to walk off trails — You can explore the park freely if you obey a few rules: If you are close to a trail, walk on it. Respect areas marked as closed by a sign, usually done to protect or restore nature.

9. It is allowed to enter fenced areas — Their purpose is to protect the plants from the many elk and study the growth of the flora, not to keep people out.

10. Be friendly to everyone — Being friendly is easier for everyone. It's especially kind to the many park officials and volunteers, who dedicate a lot of their time so you can enjoy a clean environment, healthy wildlife and a well maintained infrastructure.

Elk on Trail Ridge Road

Rocky Mountain National Park

Jewel of the Rockies — that sums up what the park is. Here was preserved, what was settled elsewhere. Here was made accessible, what remains hidden in other places. The rugged beauty of the Backbone of North America is at its best here. From two towns on the east and west end of the park — Estes Park and Grand Lake — visitors can enter the alpine wonderland. A paved pass road, peaking above 12,000 feet, makes both ends meet. In between is everything you would expect in a mountain paradise: stormy peaks, wildflower-filled meadows, rapid streams, lots of trees and an abundance of wildlife.

The park is open year-round all day long. And it's as popular among visitors from all over the world as it is with locals. Hundreds of destinations with more than 360 miles of trails, some paved and accessible for everyone, others way out in the backcountry, make it one, if not *the* premier hiking place among our national parks. But there is something for everyone in the park. Kids will love the many animals in the park — from big to small — and even people bound to their car can enjoy the beautiful scenery. But whenever possible, small hikes bring you even closer to the many wonders of the park.

This book will guide you through the park and give you a lot of options on what to do and see. Use it like a menu in a restaurant — take a look at what's offered and choose whatever you like best. For your convenience we have divided the park into four regions, that can all be reached by car. Since the majority of visitors come from the eastern side, meaning Estes Park, our directions start from that side. But you can just as easily use them coming from Grand Lake in the west — just look at the two chapters on Trail Ridge Road backwards, starting with the last stop.

Besides from the parts describing the different regions you will find chapters giving you background information on what else you need to know in order to plan your trip and what you might encounter in the park. We suggest that you review this information before you come to visit the park. This way, you don't need to take precious time away from your vacation — and you can even start the vacation early in your mind by enjoying our beautiful pictures. We have kept the parts on general touristic information to a minimum, so that there is more about the park itself. Estes Park (visitestespark.com) offers all there needs to be from lodging and shopping to dining. And the metropolitan area of the Colorado Front Range around Denver is only an hour away. Grand Lake (grandlakechamber.com) on the west side of the park is more quiet and remote and there are less amenities, but it's a great place to camp and enjoy the outdoors.

One word of advice: if you're coming from out of state, take a day or two to adapt. Colorado is all about altitude. Denver is already a mile high (exactly 5,280 feet) and if you come by plane, you might notice that you need to take a deep breath when you step out of the plane. The entrance to the park in Estes Park is even higher at 7,500 feet. Let your body get accustomed to the altitude and it's lower oxygen content.

This book is a guide for everyone who wants to explore the park on a short vacation. And even if you stay longer, it's a good start, pointing you to many things you can see, do and enjoy in the park. Use the park's website (nps.gov/romo) to complement it and get the latest updates. Use this book to get the most out of your visit. Even if you come only for one day — the park is well worth it.

Left: View of Longs Peak, Half Mountain and Thatchtop from Bierstadt Moraine (left to right)

Directions

The park has two main directions from which it can be entered. On its eastern side lies the town of Estes Park, which has two entrances close by. The west entrance is located in Grand Lake. The two sides are connected by U.S. Highway 34 which runs through the park, and is open between June and early October. Both towns are oriented towards serving visitors coming to the park all year long. Neither town is big, but Estes Park is larger than Grand Lake.

Estes Park can be reached from the Denver area by U.S. Highway 36. Coming from the Colorado Front Range around Denver this will usually be the entry-point of choice with a driving time of about one and a half hours. The two entrances are about 4 miles west of the town center. The northern entrance is served by U.S. Highway 34, the southern by U.S. Highway 36. Both highways run together in the town center, but split up on either side of town. They merge again in the park becoming U.S. Highway 34.

The western entrance of the park is directly at the north end of the town of Grand Lake. Located 15 miles south of Grand Lake on U.S. Highway 34 is Granby, which is a bit larger and offers additional amenities. This is a winter sports region, making it the area of choice for tourists in the wintertime. Granby is connected to Interstate 70 by U.S. Highway 40 going through the Rocky Mountains. Interstate 70 connects Denver and the Front Range Urban Corridor with the western part of Colorado including Vail, Aspen and Grand Junction before heading into Utah. If you're coming from Utah, this is the shortest way into the park. The drive from Denver on the western route is — depending on your location — usually longer than the eastern and takes about two hours.

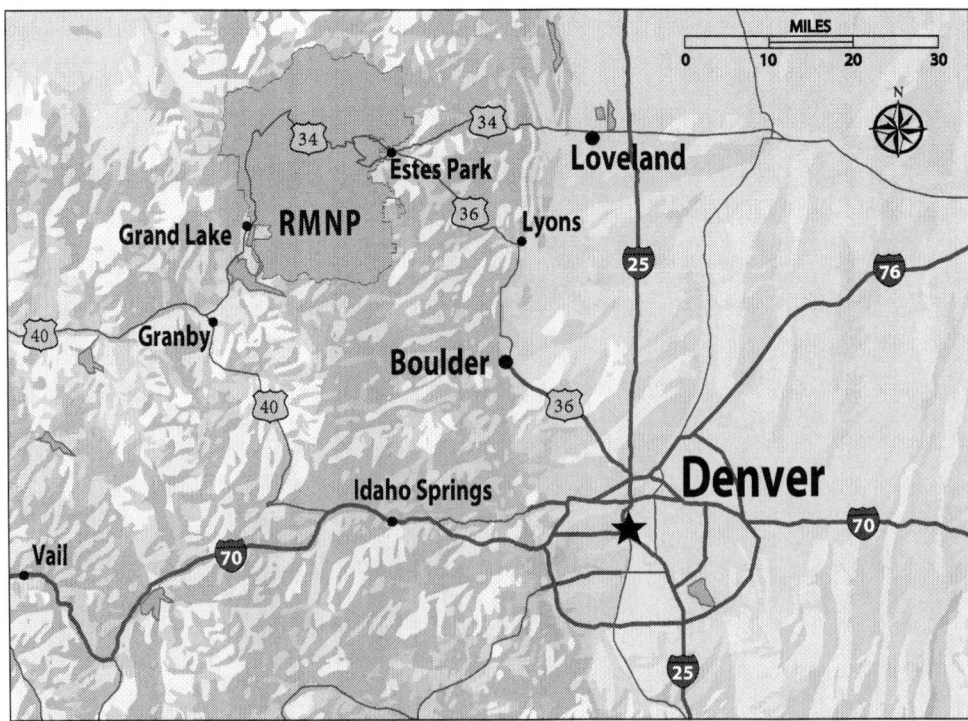

Entrance Fees

Like most national parks Rocky Mountain National Park charges an entrance fee. For cars, including all passengers, it's $20 per week. Pedestrians and bikers pay $10 per person for a week. A good alternative, if you're doing a round-trip with several parks, can be the so called Interagency Annual Pass. It's valid for national parks and other recreational lands overseen by federal agencies. At $80 for one year, it's granting access for one car including all passengers. For locals a $40 annual pass just for Rocky Mountain National Park or $50 including the Arapaho National Recreation Area is available. Also lifetime passes for seniors at $10 (must be 62 or older and a U.S. citizen or permanent resident) or for free for permanently disabled people are available. Unfortunately the National Park Service has announced that it plans to increase the prices for many of its parks in 2015. For Rocky Mountain National Park an increase of 50% is planned.

Visitor Centers

Rocky Mountain National Park has a total of five visitor centers which are marked in the overview map on page 40 and the map that you get when visiting the park. Three of these are on the eastern side near Estes Park. One is on the western side just north of Grand Lake and the last one is in the middle of the park along Trail Ridge Road. Each visitor center offers restrooms and different other amenities. The three visitor centers on the eastern side are Beaver Meadows Visitor Center, Fall River Visitor Center and Moraine Park Visitor Center. Fall River Visitor Center has the largest gift shop in the park as well as a cafe and an exhibition where you can take a close look at the animals in the park — as brass statues. Beaver Meadows Visitor Center is closest to Estes Park and shows a 20-minute film about the park. Moraine Park Visitor Center has a small museum. Alpine Visitor Center has a cafeteria and Kawuneeche Visitor Center also shows the 20-minute movie. A bookstore can be found in every visitor center.

You don't have to stop at every visitor center. Just make sure to stop at one of them when going into the park to catch up on the latest information. Also the rangers will be happy

Fall River Visitor Center exhibit

Moraine Park Visitor Center

to answer any questions you might have and you can check the schedule of ranger-led programs that you might want to attend. To get the most out of your visit, stop at Fall River Visitor Center for the large gift shop and the exhibition. Also you will likely stop at Alpine Visitor Center and if it's only for the restrooms. If you're coming from Grand Lake you might want to consider stopping at Kawuneeche Visitor Center instead of the Fall River Visitor Center to get some vacation souvenirs.

Lodging & Campgrounds

Both sides of the park, namely the towns of Estes Park, Grand Lake, and Granby, offer accommodations for tourists. In and around Estes Park are lots of small and large hotels, motels and campgrounds. Restaurants and stores make sure, that nobody has to go to sleep hungry. Also Granby and Grand Lake offer accommodations, albeit at a slightly smaller level. But here as well nobody will starve and everybody should be able to find a bed for the night. However, during the prime season in the summer you're well advised to book in advance. Also, the western side provides some skiing areas right by, so it can become crowded in the winter, too, while giving you more choices on what to do at the same time. Prices are reasonable in both towns, considering they are tourist destinations.

For those of you who are camping, there are five nice campgrounds within the park. All are open for tents, but if you're RVing, only four campgrounds will be able to accommodate you. Two of them take up to 30 feet long vehicles, the other two go up to 35 feet and 40 feet respectively. There a no hookups in the park, but three of the campgrounds in the park offer a potable water refill and a sewer dump station during the summer. For details please see the park's website. Also the towns around the park offer great accommodations for RVers. If you're bringing a large RV, you should be comfortable driving it, if you want to cross the park on the steep and winding Trail Ridge Road. It's doable, but it will require full concentration and likely not feel like a leisure trip.

The Timber Creek Campground

Shuttle Bus

The park maintains a free of charge shuttle bus system on the eastern side, mainly serving the areas around Bear Lake Road. Since many great hiking trails lie in this region, the parking lots there get crowded early on and the shuttle bus helps to ease this. This

is especially true for the Bear Lake and the Fern Lake Trailhead parking lots. The shuttle bus gets you there worry and cost free. The bus is also a great way for hikers to make one-way trips. Park your car at the end of your trail and use the shuttle bus to get to the trailhead — or vice versa. This comes in especially handy when the way back is going way up.

Shuttle bus at work

In total there are three routes running on regular schedules. The Moraine Park Route is going to the Fern Lake Trailhead and the Bear Lake Route is going to Bear Lake. Both start from the large Park & Ride parking lot about half-way down the Bear Lake Road. The buses operate between 7 a.m. and 7 p.m. every day from mid-June to mid-October. Between Memorial Day weekend and mid-June they run only on weekends. The third route is an express service that connects the Estes Park Visitor Center, located in the town of Estes Park, to the Park & Ride parking lot and thus to the other two shuttle bus lines. It runs from 6:30 a.m. to 7:30 p.m. from the end of June to early September. After that it only runs on weekends until mid-October. Our tip is to use the shuttle bus in the morning when possible and park your car at the end of your trail — this way you don't need to watch the clock in the evening.

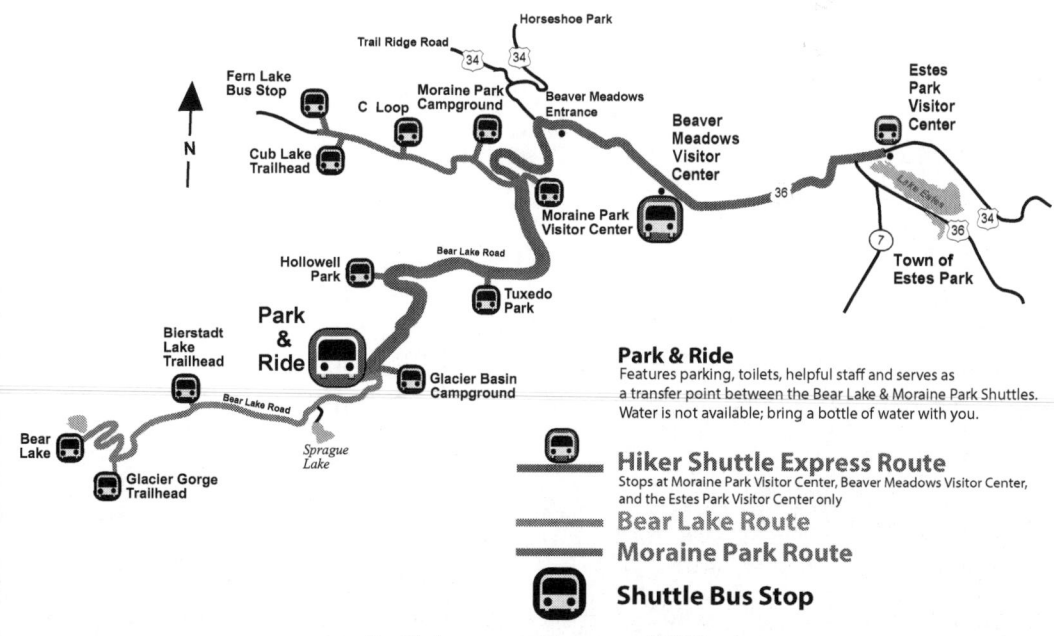

Shuttle bus routes (Courtesy of NPS)

ACTIVITIES

Only your imagination limits the possibilities to explore the park. Whether it's just one or a few days in the park, there are some typical activities you should consider. We present them in more detail on the following pages. They will be fun to do and connect you and your family to the nature around you as well as give you a deeper understanding of history, geology, wildlife and survival in Rocky Mountain National Park.

All the activities are outdoors, so please check the weather ahead of time. All visitor centers display the current forecast. Please respect the few rules that have been established for your safety and the well being of the park. Enjoy and embrace the wonders of the park.

Ranger-Led Programs

Rocky Mountain National Park offers ranger-led programs year-round. The programs are free of charge and a great opportunity to get first hand information. Obviously there are more programs in the summer, because the visitor numbers peak here, but even in the wintertime there are some things to do in the park. You can find current information on the programs at the park's website or at any visitor center. Except for the winter programs, reservations are usually not required. You just drop-in at the starting time and enjoy.

The range of activities reaches from explanatory talks and walks to science and wildlife watching. An important part are the kids programs, especially the Junior Ranger program (see section "Fun for Kids"). The rangers are usually doing a great job, being full of knowledge, but also finding the right mix of how to explain things and motivate their audience. Our suggestion: try at least one of the programs.

A ranger explains how to use a map

Driving by Car

Like most national parks in the lower 48 states, Rocky Mountain National Park is easily accessible by car. While some parts are designated and will remain wilderness, there are many great places in the park that can be reached by car. One can easily spend all day seeing different exciting things and almost never leave the car.

U.S. Highway 34 — in the park known as Trail Ridge Road — runs right through the park including the scenic wonderland of the alpine tundra. It connects Estes Park in the east with Grand Lake in the west. Another road, Bear Lake Road, connects to the hiking region in the southern part of the park. Also the old road up to the alpine tundra, Old Fall River Road, provides visitors with a steep one-way gravel road adventure. Several smaller roads in the eastern part of the park give access to special features in the meadows region.

Left: Glacier Creek at the Sprague Lake Trailhead

Guided Tours

If you want to relax and still get to see the wonders of the park, a guided tour might be the right thing for you. There are all kinds of tours, ranging from sightseeing to photography as well as hiking and horseback riding. Since the tours are privately organized, they cannot be found on the park's website. However, you can find them at visitestespark.com and grandlakechamber.com, where you can also find visitor guides. Or you just look around in town once you get there.

The sightseeing tours are usually done in an open Jeep, with a guide telling you all there is to know about the different parts of the park. The tour will stop at important locations, giving you the opportunity to take pictures. The Jeep tours are for example a good choice for those, who do not want to drive the steep and unpaved Old Fall River Road by themselves.

Horseback Riding

Rocky Mountain National Park is a horseback rider's paradise. There are 260 miles of trails which can be explored on a horse's back. Eight concessionaires offer guided tours in the park. Most of them have stables in and around Estes Park while others are located in Grand Lake or within the park. Since they are concessionaires, you will find their names on the park's website.

The tours offer something for everybody, even if you have never been on a horse before. The guided tours are ranging from one hour to a full day and are especially fun for families. You can also bring your own horse to the park — as well as mules, ponies, llamas and burros, which are all allowed on park trails. However, there are some restrictions on which trails can be used, so make sure to check with the rangers before you unleash your mount.

Horseback riding in the Horseshoe Park area

The hike to Dream Lake is popular. Come early or out of season to be alone.

Hiking

Hiking is probably the main activity in the park — be it just a few feet to a pristine lake or a scenic overlook or miles and miles out in the backcountry, sleeping in a tent. Along the car routes lie many short trails that make it easy to explore the beauty of the mountains even if one is not an avid hiker.

Throughout this book you will find many examples and recommended hikes, most of them fairly easy to do, wearing sneakers, even for families and the elderly. However, for all longer hikes you should consider wearing hiking boots with sturdy soles. Your and your children's feet will thank you. There are also several scenic trails that are wheelchair accessible. Some are mentioned in this book, especially Bear Lake, Sprague Lake and Coyote Valley Trail. Details are described on the park's website.

Jogging

If you want to take it to the extreme, why not run up the mountains? It's mostly locals who are used to the altitude, who challenge themselves this way. But if you consider yourself to be in need of some extra training, feel free to join in. Exercising at this high altitude will boost the amount of oxygen your blood can transport, giving you an advantage for a few weeks after your return to the flatlands. So it comes at no surprise, that quite a few renowned athletes live and train in Colorado. When you come to the park for more than a few days, you can increase the altitude from day to day to get the most out of it. The most popular trails for jogging are well maintained hiking trails in the Moraine Park and the Bear Lake region. If you're looking for less busy trails consider the west side along the Kawuneeche Valley.

Backcountry Hiking and Camping

Rocky Mountain National Park is arguably the best park to hike in the lower 48 states. You can basically hike anywhere you want in the park including the backcountry, i.e. the unmarked wilderness. This may include overnight camping. To go into the backcountry you should be well prepared, having laid out a route ahead of time and carrying supplies. Also a map and a compass are a must, ideally supplemented by a GPS device.

If you plan an overnight hike in the backcountry you have to stop at the backcountry office to get the required backcountry camping permit. On the east side, the office is located next to the Beaver Meadows Visitor Center. On the west side it's in the Kawuneeche Valley Visitor Center. There is also a backcountry camping guide for download from the park's website.

Climbing

Technical climbing is already an ambitious sport just by itself. But doing it in the heights of the Rockies is yet another experience, especially when it's not an everyday venture for you. Rocky Mountain National Park gives you plenty of opportunities to climb, from easy walls to challenging multi-day climbs on big walls. Day use requires no permit, but overnight climbs will require a bivouac permit. Even if you are new to climbing, the park offers a chance to learn it through guided trips by the park concessionaire Colorado Mountain School (coloradomountainschool.com).

Different locations are popular for climbing in the park. Lumpy Ridge at the northern border of Estes Park is very popular due to it's wide range of difficulties and great views. However, it can be very crowded, so climbing here on weekdays is recommended. Cathedral Wall above The Loch lake is another favorite place for climbers.

When climbing, please follow the unwritten rules local climbers and the rangers have come up with to ensure, that climbing in the park will be an adventure for generations to come. The basic principle is the same as always in national parks: leave no trace, meaning clean-climbing techniques. The park's website tells you more.

Painting

Moraine Park scenery

Everyone has a different perception on how he sees the park. Painting is a way to express this view. The Rocky Mountain National Park offers an inspiring surrounding which elevates emotions that want to be painted. Albert Bierstadt e.g. has become famous for his paintings of the American West, yet he also received criticism because of his too romantic views. Now his paintings are even hanging in the White House. And in the park a lake, a mountain and a moraine are named after him. Today painters from everywhere come to the park to catch a glimpse of this fantastic world on canvas. What do you feel when you are in the park? How do you express it?

Winter-Activities

Rocky Mountain National Park is open year round. However, the main activities change in the winter. When the alpine wonderland is covered with snow, cross-country skiing, snowshoeing and sledding replace hiking as the favorite pastime. If you need some starting up on winter activities, you might want to join a ranger-led program. Different programs offer beginner and intermediate level snowshoeing and cross-country skiing on both sides of the park.

However, in the winter you must decide ahead of time, which part of the park you will visit, since Trail Ridge Road is closed. Coming from Estes Park the park offers many opportunities for the ambitious snowshoe hiker and cross-country skier to enjoy the magical winter wonderlands of Horseshoe Park, Moraine Park and the Bear Lake Region. The latter is possible, because Bear Lake

Snowshoeing

Road stays open year-round. Favorite winter destinations are Cub Lake and Bear Lake. Going closer to the mountainsides, e.g. to The Loch or Mills Lake, requires some tracking skills and stamina. Depending on the conditions it might also be a good idea to bring an avalanche safety gear. Coming from the winter sports region near Grand Lake the park offers similar opportunities in the Kawuneeche Valley in front of the majestic Never Summer Mountains. Especially tours along the Colorado River are popular. And remember: you don't need to follow a fixed trail, but could e.g. follow a frozen creek.

Another fun activity is to watch wildlife in the wintertime. Especially large mammals like elk and moose are easy to spot in the otherwise white terrain. The best spots to see them remain the same as in the summer: moose are easiest to find in the Kawuneeche Valley, elk and deer in all the meadow-lands. Several birds winter in the park and all the small critters are around as well. Some as the snowshoe hares and the white-tailed ptarmigans even change their fur or feathers to a snowy white.

Weather Watching

Weather can change fast in Rocky Mountain National Park, giving you the opportunity to watch it. The Coyote Valley Trail e.g. is a great place to watch a distant thunderstorm developing over the Never Summer Mountains. The alpine tundra on the other hand often receives snow as early as September. A cool morning or evening might bring the first snowfall to watch.

But weather has its risks. Lightning should be taken very serious in the mountains. In the park two people were killed in two events in July 2014, one even close to his car at Rainbow Curve. Seek shelter, when a thunderstorm approaches you. A rule of thumb: when thunder and lightning appear less than 30 seconds apart, you can be struck.

Lightning illuminates the clouds

Fun for Kids

What is more heart-warming than the happy glance of children's eyes when they discover the world? The park offers many opportunities for kids to have fun and learn about nature, cultural aspects and history at the same time — and not only about the park but also about the discovery of the West. They learn to respect and appreciate what nature has to offer.

A ranger explains the bighorn sheep's abilities to survive

The Moraine Park Visitor Center has a hands-on exhibition, which is a great place to start with your kids. The museum is mostly interactive and lets the kids turn dials and pull levers to change the land, simulating the impact of glaciers, climate and other geological factors. They will for example see how a glacier creates a moraine.

Many of the ranger-led programs are also specifically aimed at children. They teach various things about the park. And because the rangers are usually very enthusiastic and charming, the kids are having lots of fun. For example they get to see and touch furs, skulls and antlers of animals and learn, how they help the animals to survive the elements. Also there is a Junior Ranger program, where the kids have to finish tasks from an activity book and then are officially rewarded with a Junior Ranger badge. Aimed at children between 5 and 13, the whole family gets to participate and share the fun. Depending on the age, the kids get booklets with different tasks. Parents can get more information about the Junior Ranger program and take a look at the booklets on the park's website.

Bicycling

Bicycles in the park are limited to roads and are not allowed on trails or off-road. However, the park offers more than 60 miles of roads on which bikes are allowed with grades up to 7 degrees. Most challenging of all, the Trail Ridge Road leads you up to 12,183 feet, guaranteeing for burning legs. But prepare your ride well. Cycling to the top of the Trail Ridge Road is said to be one of the two toughest rides in Colorado. The other of the two is the road up Mount Evans, one of the two 14ers in the state that has a road going all the way up to the summit.

When riding in the park, bring warm clothes with you and have an eye on the weather. Thunderstorms are rolling in on many afternoons and they develop quickly in the mountains, giving you not much of a heads-up. Starting early will help you avoid this as well as crowds, that form during the day especially on summer weekends.

During winter most of the Trail Ridge Road is closed. But there are some opportunities to bike, most prominently on Bear Lake Road, that is plowed all winter long. Trail Ridge Road opens in spring a few weeks earlier for bicycles than it opens for motor vehicles. This gives the ambitious biker the opportunity to cross the park and embrace nature in silence without hindering or being hindered by cars.

Fishing

Fishing in a national park? No problem in Rocky Mountain National Park, as long as you have a valid Colorado fishing license. You can buy it in many stores, including several fishing and sporting goods stores in Estes Park. For non-residents a year-long license is $66 in 2014 (the license year starts on April 1st), while a 5-day license is $31.

Both prices include a mandatory $10 habitat stamp that you need to buy as well. For short trips you can buy a daily license for $9 and one additional day for $5 without the habitat stamp.

Brook trout in the Fall River

In the park waters live different kinds of trouts and suckers. Some of them are native, while others were stocked in the park's early days. Depending on the lake you may take your catch home or must do catch-and-release, while some lakes are off-limits for anglers and others don't even have fish. If you catch one of the endangered greenback cutthroat trouts, you must always release it. Usually there are signs telling you what is allowed and, of course, you can always ask the friendly rangers. There is also an information sheet that tells you all about the rules for download on the park's website.

Picnicking

There are many opportunities in the park to sit down, stretch your legs and enjoy nature while picnicking with friends and family. While there is lots of traffic in most picnic areas on the east side of the park, the less crowded west side offers a different, more quiet picnic experience.

The picnic areas we recommend are Sprague Lake, Hollowell Park and Hidden Valley (especially the tables along the trail) on the east side and Lake Irene, Beaver Creek & Ponds as well as Coyote Valley on the west side of the park.

Picnic site at
Hidden Valley Trail

Take a Break

Why not enjoy nature while taking a nap in a hammock? Find yourself some sturdy trees and enjoy the sounds of nature around you. Overnight hikers have long discovered this method of sleeping comfortably in the wilderness. But remember: don't harm the trees and be bear aware!

Another way to take a break in the park is to lie down in one of the many meadows. On dry days they make good mattresses. A short nap may bring back some energy you just spent on a long hike. Good to know that there are no poisonous snakes in the park.

Sleeping visitor in a hammock

Photography

Rocky Mountain National Park is a great place to practice your photography skills. Almost every visitor takes at least a few pictures, using devices ranging from smartphones to professional gear. The park offers many great opportunities for taking pictures in different areas of photography. Especially landscape enthusiasts are served well. But also lovers of fast moving objects will like chasing after the parks birds and critters. Portrait photographers will obviously take pictures of their families, but also can practice on some of the wildlife that comes pretty close — albeit without studio lights.

There is neither one kind of photography nor a single hint, that will catch it all. Therefore we have used the regions section of this book to hint to great locations for scenic pictures and where to find certain animals. No matter, what kind of camera you have, the park has something for you to capture. And of course everybody has a different sense of art. So you might take a totally different picture of the "Grandma Tree" on the left side of this page than we did.

The different seasons obviously yield different pictures, but no season is better than the others — all have their beauty. What matters more is the time of day. Morning and evening usually give you a better light and also the chance of meeting animals is better than in bright sunshine. So get up early, take a siesta at noon and stay up late in order to get the most out of a photographer's day. Also consider where the sun and probably even the moon stand during the different times of the day, so you have them in the right place for that panoramic shot. To determine this in advance we recommend you use a sun and moon calculator, available both web-based and as a mobile app.

Wildlife Viewing

The park is a great place to watch wildlife, be it large or small, be it airborne, grounded or even swimming. There are some basic things you should keep in mind, when watching wildlife in the park. First of all they are wild animals, not pets. So none of the animals can be petted. They may be used to humans, but that doesn't mean they care much for us. Larger animals should not be approached too closely, especially when they have offspring, or they might charge you. Also you should never feed the animals. They might get poisoned or get addicted to being fed and will not be able to take care of themselves.

The large predators — mountain lions and black bears — are seldom seen by visitors. If you run into them, retreat facing them, make yourself large and make noise. When trying to get closer to wildlife, you should do the opposite: stay quiet, try to be invisible and approach against the wind. Your chance of getting that close-up will be greatly enhanced. Also, some of the animals can be heard first. This might give you a clue where to look. Hummingbirds e.g. sound like cicadas. Once you figured this sound out, they are pretty easy to spot. Finally, always look for animals you want to find in their usual places first. The regions section later in the book will tell you, where these places are.

Sheep report at
Sheep Lakes

Left: "The Grandma Tree" is one of the oldest trees in the park. It greets hikers at Lake Haiyaha.

Rainbow and sunbeam over McGregor Mountain

NATURE

It's all about nature in Rocky Mountain National Park. Wildlife, vegetation, climate and geology all contribute to the incredibly versatile and beautiful natural scenery.

Weather and Seasons

Rocky Mountain National Park has four distinct seasons. Each of them offers a lot to visitors and the park is open year round. The main tourist season is summer when pleasant temperatures are reached, even at higher altitudes. Estes Park at 7,500 feet, for example, has a median high in the upper 70s in July and August, and even days in June and September usually reach 70 degrees Fahrenheit. At the same time outside of the mountains, in the plains around Denver, it gets really hot with average highs in July and August close to 90 degrees. However, due to the altitude, the temperature variation between day and night is high and the temperature drops about 30 degrees at night.

Also the altitude has a strong influence on the temperature. As a rule of thumb the temperature drops 3 to 5 degrees for every 1,000 feet. Therefore the highest peaks at 14,000 feet, even in July usually don't reach more than the mid 50s and drop below the freezing point at night. The highest road in the park, Trail Ridge Road, climbs to more than 12,000 feet close to the Alpine Visitor Center. In July and August the temperature will usually only go up to 60 degrees. Taking the strong winds up there into consideration, a jacket should be part of your equipment.

During spring and fall the temperatures are significantly lower than in the summer. May and October see temperatures around 60 degrees in the lower altitudes, while the alpine parts of the park receive the first or last snow. Trail Ridge Road usually closes in mid-October for the year and re-opens in June. Don't miss the fall foliage in Rocky Mountain National Park. In early September the aspen trees start to turn golden and especially the Bear Lake area looks enchanted. This coincides with the elk rut and still pleasant temperatures, making it a great time to visit the park.

In the wintertime the whole park is covered with snow. However, the lower altitudes stay accessible year round for activities like hiking and snow-shoeing. Due to the much lower number of visitors it often feels like having the park for oneself. The temperatures at the lower elevations during the winter are actually higher than you may suspect. Estes Park often reaches the upper 30s from December to February and the strong sun helps to keep you warm. Some days even reach 50 degrees, while others stay well below freezing. But at night it can get bitterly cold with temperatures from zero to under minus 30 degrees.

Besides the temperature, three other factors need to be considered when planning a trip to Colorado. Number one is the humidity. Unlike the East Coast, Colorado has a very dry climate, making the same temperatures in summer and winter feel more comfortable than in humid climates. At the same time the water consumption rises. Locals can often be identified by the water bottle they carry around, even when walking in town. On hikes you should carry at least one quart of water for each person. The water in streams and lakes unfortunately is not potable due to microorganisms that cause diarrhea. The second factor is the sun. Due to the latitude and the altitude the sun is extremely strong. Sunscreen is advised year round. The third reasons is the rapidly changing weather at higher altitudes. During summer thunderstorms often form in the afternoon, making it a good choice to start the day early. Lightning can be especially dangerous above the treeline. Climbing to lower elevations or seeking shelter in the car are highly advised when a thunderstorm approaches. In 2014 two people were killed by lightning in Rocky Mountain National Park and many more were injured.

Ecosystems

The manifold vegetation and rich wildlife of the park live in four distinct ecosystems. Their upper and lower limits vary depending on weather and soil conditions. The given numbers here are rough estimates.

Upper montane ecosystem: The upper montane zone from 7,800 to 9,100 feet contains mostly meadows and forests. Meadows dominate where, e.g. at the bottom of valleys, the soil is too wet to support trees. Aspen, Douglas fir, ponderosa pine and lodgepole pine are the most common trees. Streams meander through the open parklands, providing water for the plentiful wildlife in this zone. Mule deer, elk, coyotes, bobcats, mountain lions and many other mammals can be found here as well as birds like the great-horned owl, northern goshawk and broad-tailed hummingbird.

Subalpine ecosystem: From 9,100 to 11,500 feet the subalpine zone is dominated by a spruce-fir forest made up mainly of Engelmann spruce and subalpine fir. Where fires recently raged, mostly lodgepole pines will be found. The trees are often hundreds of years old and up to 100 feet tall. Due to the long lasting snow in this zone, the forests are humid and cool. These dark rugged forests shelter more animals than one would expect. American martens, chickarees, porcupines and weasels are among them.

Krummholz transition: Beginning at about 11,000 feet the harsh weather leaves its marks on the trees. They are small, wind beaten, dry, crippled and appear to be almost dead. However, these strange looking trees are hundreds of years old. They are called Krummholz and mark the transition between the subalpine and the alpine ecosystem.

Alpine ecosystem: 11,500 feet mark in the park the treeline above which trees cannot survive. Above it, the parts with richer soil are dominated by grasses and wildflowers, while mosses and lichens cover rocks and meager soil. They cramp themselves to the ground, withstanding winds that can be 150 miles-per-hour strong. All plants in the tundra have deep roots. This helps them to outlast the strong winds and also keeps the precious soil in place. The plants also have built-in protection systems. Chemicals function as anti-freeze while hairy stems and leaves protect the plants from cooling down. Many small creatures have also adapted to survive in this harsh climate.

Riparian habitat: These are the riversides and wetlands of the park. These lush areas show the most diversity of all the ecosystems in the park. They are usually easy to spot as a band of aspen, willows and other deciduous trees. In spring and summer their green is much lighter than the dark green of the conifers, while in fall and winter they obviously look completely different from the evergreens. Sedges and grasses grow along the streams and lakes, while fish and myriads of insects cavort in the waters. Animals small and large come to the water to drink and feed on the rich vegetation.

Fall colors in the Rocky Mountains: golden aspen near Bear Lake frame Hallett Peak

Dusky grouse at Fern Lake Trail

Golden-mantled ground squirrel

Bighorn ewe with lambs

Bighorn ram

Yellow-bellied marmots

Bull elk

Chickaree

American pika gathering winter stocks

Animals

Rocky Mountain National Park is vibrant with life that has adapted perfectly to the rough conditions in the mountains. Both large and small animals can be spotted in many places. Due to the different life zones, varying animals can be spotted, depending on the altitude you are at. Both the forests below the tree line and the tundra above provide space to dwell for many species.

Almost everywhere in the park you will be able to watch large herbivores, foremost elk (also called wapiti). They are large deer, roaming the meadows and forests. Due to a lack of natural predators in the park, there are now several thousand elk living in the park and they are a common sight, usually grazing in small groups. Outside of the rut either only bulls or cows are in a group. The impressive animals can weigh up to 900 pounds, yet still run up to 35 mph. The bulls sport large antlers, that are grown anew every year. Their little cousins, the mule deer, can also be found in the park. They are less common and much smaller, but still beautiful animals with oversized ears, which gave them their name.

Larger in size than elk in the park are only moose. They are the largest members of the deer family and were re-introduced to the area in 1978/79, when a few animals were set free west of the Never Summer Mountains. They quickly became frequent visitors to the Kawuneeche Valley and later permanent residents. Different from elk, who prefer groups, the moose usually roam the meadows alone or in same sex pairs.

Another large ungulate in the park are the bighorn sheep. However, they mostly live up in the mountains and only come down to the lowlands in order to feed on sediments to balance their mineral intake. Until the mid-1800s thousands of these impressive animals roamed the park. When the settlers came to the mountains, their numbers started to decrease due to hunting, diseases and shrinking habitats. At the lowest point only about 140 sheep remained in the park, while today their number has gone up to 350.

Cow elk nibbling on wild berries

There are also several predators roaming the park, even though the two strongest, wolves and grizzlies, became extinct in Colorado a long time ago. Common in the park are coyotes, though due to being active a night, they are not a common sight. They hunt in packs like their larger cousins, the wolves, and their nightly howls sometimes create a special kind of serenade. Much less common are black bears, which are actually omnivores, feeding both on smaller animals and plants. Like other predators they usually avoid contact with humans. This is even more the case with another large predator living in the park. The mountain lions (also known as cougars) are impressive cats, but hardly ever seen by visitors. They pray on animals up to younger or sick elk and moose, but prefer mule deer. Smaller predators, like bobcats and long-tailed weasels, are also living in the park, taking care of the populations of smaller herbivores and fish.

There are quite a few smaller herbivores living in the park, many of them being a common sight. Small, hard to spot due to his camouflaged fur and unique to the alpine tundra is the pika, a mouse-sized relative of rabbits. It often has a bunch of grass in its mouth, making for cute pictures. Also living up in the tundra is the yellow-bellied marmot, a large relative of the squirrels, which is almost the size of a small raccoon.

In the lower parts of the park squirrels dominate with a total of ten different species. The smallest of them is the least chipmunk, which is less than ten inches long and rather easy to identify by the typical chipmunk-stripes. The only squirrel it might be confused with is the golden-mantled ground squirrel. However, the latter is two inches larger and has the chipmunk-stripes only on the body but not on the head. Another inch larger is the chickaree or pine squirrel. Much larger and because of its black fur and ear tufts easily recognizable is Abert's squirrel, which roams the ponderosa pines.

A satyr comma flies away after feeding on an aspen daisy

Rocky Mountain parnassian

The park is home to over 250 different kinds of birds, of which most only spend one season in the park or traverse it as migratory birds during spring and fall. However, the large predatory birds usually stay all year long with the notable exception of the bald eagle, which only lives in the park in late fall and early winter. Its cousin the golden eagle lives in the park all year long, preying mostly on smaller mammals like squirrels and rabbits. Other birds of prey include turkey vultures as well as several species of hawks, falcons and owls including the great horned owl, the largest owl in North America. Like most owls it preys at night and flies without a sound, but has an easily recognizable hoot.

The park also hosts many omni- and herbivorous birds. A common sight are magpies, which are smart birds that usually are not very shy of humans. Another pretty and fairly common bird is the Steller's jay, whose upper half is black including a Mohawk-style headdress while the lower half is a vibrant blue. An impressive forest dweller is the dusky grouse. It's the second largest grouse in North America and weighs up to three pounds. Other common sights in the park include many smaller birds like hummingbirds, wrens, warblers and flycatchers. The park's website provides a list of all birds documented in the park, telling you in which season they can be seen and how common they are.

The lakes in the park shelter eleven species of fish, with the most common being trouts and suckers. Some are indigenous to the park, while others were released in the early

Atlantis fritillary

Black bear

Great horned owl

Magpie hatchling

Least chipmunk

Cow moose

Steller's jay

Coyote

days of the park for tourists to catch. Less than one third of all lakes hold fish populations that reproduce, because especially in the high altitude lakes the water temperatures are too cold and they lack spawning habitats.

Spiders and insects are also common in the park. The insects range from mosquitoes and other stinging insects to dragonflies and many different beetles. Perhaps the most pretty sight are the over 140 different species of butterflies. The park's website even has a list of the different butterflies for download. Among them are swallowtails like the Rocky Mountain parnassian and the western tiger swallowtail as well as brushfoot like the satyr commas and the Atlantis fritillary. If you have a steady hand, some patience and a lens that allows for close-ups, butterflies are also great to take pictures of.

Globeflower

Prickly rose

Black-eyed susan

Plants

The four ecosystems in Rocky Mountain National Park provide very different living conditions for plants of all kinds. From green meadows and forests in the montane zone to the hardened vegetation of the alpine tundra above the treeline and from lush wetlands in the riparian zone to sturdy Krummholz at the upper end of the subalpine forest.

The lower parts of the park in the montane zone are dominated by extensive conifer forests made up mostly of ponderosa pines and some other evergreens. Towards higher elevations more and more Douglas firs tend to be found. In between the evergreens lie spots covered by a deciduous tree, the aspen. Unlike many other trees, the aspen usually replicates itself by root sprouts instead of seeds. Therefore several, sometimes hundreds of trees in one spot originate from the same root, making them clones that look alike. This can be seen especially well in the fall, because the identical clones change colors at the same time, leading to different patches of the same colors in the forest. While the aspen leaf does not turn red, like leaves of maples and other trees in the East, it first turns yellow, then becomes almost golden before it changes to brown. It can be argued whether this beats the fall foliage on the East Coast, but the full fall foliage in the park in mid September is a truly marvelous sight.

The subalpine zone is dominated by more conifers, mostly Engelmann spruce and subalpine fir. The forest here is much denser and darker than in the montane zone, which favors those two trees

Arctic gentian

Butter-and-eggs

Scarlet paintbrush

Yellow stonecrop

Nodding onion

Blanket flower

Yellow pond-lily

Alpine columbine

because their seeds are among the few who grow in the darkness of the subalpine forest. In some places you will also spot larger stocks of lodgepole pines. They are the first to grow, when a fire has burned the subalpine forest, because their seeds like bright sunlight. Engelmann spruce and subalpine fir will take over when a forest cover has been established and the ground is once more hidden in the shadows.

Within the montane and the subalpine zone spots and bands of the riparian zone can be found along lakes and streams. This zone is vibrant with plants and wildlife. Depending on the altitude different deciduous trees like willows, alders and birches are lining the waterfront. Many flowers can be found blossoming in the rich soils as well as sappy grasses and reeds.

In the alpine zone everything grows slow and stays small. Besides small bushes and grass on the richer grounds, much of the area is covered by mosses and lichen, both providing the visitor with a very colorful scenery. The lichen, which are in fact not plants but a symbiosis of algae and fungi, produce a weak acid which slowly dissolves the rocks they grow on. This sets minerals free on which the life in the tundra depends. All the plants in the tundra take long to grow, because of the adverse conditions and the short growing season. A small bush may be hundreds of years old, while some lichen species can live several thousands of years. Knowing this, it is understandable that once tundra life is destroyed it may take 500 to 1000 years to recover.

A colorful spectacle can be seen every year in the meadows of the montane zone as well as in the alpine zone. This event is the blossoming of the wildflowers, which first starts in late spring in the montane zone and later in the short summer up in the alpine tundra. All in all the different ecosystems in the park harbor hundreds of different wildflower species. Many millions of bees and other insects take care, that the blossoms get pollinated while harvesting their nectar. At the same time, it's a spectacle for the observer's eye as well as the photographer's lens.

Piled up wood from dead pine-trees

The pine trees in the park have been under attack by a persistent plague for the last years. The mountain pine beetle destroys ponderosa and lodgepole pines. Affected trees can easily be identified, because their needles have turned brown, giving the trees a dead look. Since these trees are also much dryer than normal, the already high risk of forest fires in the park is even higher in areas with many infested trees. Because of this, trees destroyed by the beetles are lumbered in some parts of the park and stacked in large piles on the roadside. When the weather conditions are right, they are burned in place to prevent wildfires. Well known and especially large trees are even treated with insecticides — contrary to the common principle in national parks not to interfere with nature.

The Rut

Every year in the fall the three thousand Rocky Mountain elk of the park are performing a spectacle for the visitors. Lasting most of September into early October, the rut is one of the main attractions of the park. The bull elk will try to attract and gather as many cow elk as possible. They achieve this by bugling, which is a quite impressive sound rising over more than three octaves. Once the cow elk have come closer, the bull elk start herding them using their impressive bodies. If other bull elk come too close, the antlers go into action and the two opponents start wrestling. The number of points on their antlers represents their physical shape and health, so that only the strongest bulls have a good chance with the ladies and get to spread their genes.

A strong 12-pointer with one of his cows

Great viewing areas for the rut are the meadows in the lower altitudes of the park, especially Moraine Park on the east side along the Fern Lake Road. If you're coming from the west side of the park, the Kawuneeche Valley will be a good starting point, especially the Holzwarth and Harbison meadows. Depending on the temperatures some elk will also still be grazing on the alpine meadows above the treeline. So you might be able to watch the rut from Trail Ridge Road as well. Park rangers and volunteers will close off the main meadows during the evening hours of the rut for pedestrians. But there is no need to rush. Usually visitors will be able to find a parking spot along the roadside and watch the show from there. Don't forget to bring photo and video camera. Together with the spectacular fall foliage the rut is a great reason to come to the park in September.

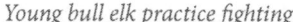
Young bull elk practice fighting

Geology

This section gives you an overview, which geological forces shaped the park and where the effects can still be seen. Details for landmarks displaying one of the effects are not noted here, but in the respective section within the regions part of this book.

The geology of Rocky Mountain National Park has undergone several phases that had different impacts on the way the park looks today. The oldest phase was the creation of the Rocky Mountains itself by plate tectonics. The Rockies were lifted up over a period of 30 million years, starting 70 million years in the past. They are the longest mountain barrier in the world and are also known as the Backbone of North America. This uplift created the granite mountains we see today, with some parts being made up of gneiss or schist. The uplift also caused volcanism emanating from large magma chambers underneath the mountains. The Never Summer Mountains were volcanoes back then, towering several thousand feet above today's range and erupting about 25 million years ago. Their magma can still be found in different places in the park today, e.g. at the Lava Cliffs and the Crater. The Front Range — the first range of the Rocky Mountains in Colorado — was lifted up by several thousand feet as the last event during the oldest phase about three million years ago.

Right after that, in geological terms, the middle phase shaped much of today's park surface during several ice ages over the last three million years. Mighty glaciers were created and melted again, creeping down mountainsides and carving the rock. As a result we see many formations of glacial origin in the park. The moraines (see section

The Tyndall Glacier shines between the granite Hallett Peak (left) and Flattop Mountain (right)

"Moraine Park") are one of them, marking the path of a glacier by deposits of rocks and soil. They show a U-shape, while valleys formed by a river display a V-shape. The bowl-shaped glacial cirques that can be seen at mountainsides (see section "Alpine Visitor Center") are another formation of glacial origin.

The newest phase are ongoing events that shape details in todays park. The forces at work are mainly slow erosion by wind and water as well as sudden events like flooding and avalanches. The Alluvial Fan (see section "Alluvial Fan") is an example of a recent structure created by a flood. It was formed in 1982 when a natural dam broke and was extended by the big flood in 2013, that caused damage all over the park.

Another geological landmark of the park is the Continental Divide, which follows the ridges of the highest mountains across North America. It is crossed by Trail Ridge Road at Milner Pass. All water falling east of it flows to the Atlantic, all west of it to the Pacific. The Continental Divide is the birthplace of more than 100 rivers, the most renowned being the Colorado River. Its headwaters can be found at the La Poudre Pass between the Never Summer Mountains and Specimen Mountain at the northern park border.

Longs Peak

Longs Peak is the most prominent mountain in the park. The square shape of it's flat top and the Keyboard of the Winds, the clustered ridge which connects Longs Peak with Pagoda Mountain, make it highly distinguishable and easy to recognize. With 14,255 feet it is also the highest peak in the park and the only fourteener, accompanied by over 100 peaks which reach at least 11,000 feet.

For thousands of years Longs Peak served as a navigational mark for the native tribes as well as early expeditions. Together with Mount Meeker it can already be seen as twin peaks from the plains. Within the park it is visible from many locations on the eastern side of the park all the way up to the Alpine Visitor Center. The peak is named after Major Steven H. Longs. He was leading the so called "Long's expedition" in 1820, exploring the region between the Mississippi and the Rocky Mountains.

Longs Peak is not only prominent with spectators, but also with mountaineers. During July and August the conditions are usually so good, that the peak can be hiked without serious mountain climbing equipment. However, there is no trail that leads up to the peak and it is still a strenuous and dangerous undertaking with steep cliffs in some parts. Almost every year people loose their lives trying to climb Longs Peak. You should only attempt it, if you are really fit and well prepared. Also you should start early in the morning, even before sunrise, in order to avoid an afternoon thunderstorm.

Longs Peak is a beautiful sight, but there are many great hiking destinations in the park, that are much easier to reach. And you get a similar vista from many points on Trail Ridge Road as from the top of Longs Peak. If you want to master a 14er: two of them in Colorado are accessible by car. Mount Evans and Pikes Peak, both outside of the park.

*Longs Peak seen from
Upper Beaver Meadows*

The square, flat top of Longs Peak

*Sunset on Longs Peak as seen just west of Rock
Cut on Trail Ridge Road*

*Longs Peak, Keyboard of the Winds and Pagoda
Mountain as seen on the way to Nymph Lake*

Recognizing Mountain Tops

There are many peaks to admire in Rocky Mountain National Park. This pictorial overview shows typical silhouettes of ranges and characteristic mountains. It will help you to recognize and distinguish them while you travel around. However, some peaks may seem prominent from certain locations, but still didn't get a name because they are just part of a bigger mountain or were deemed not important enough to get named.

South view from Bierstadt morain at the Continental Divide

View north from West Horseshoe Park Overlook

View from Rainbow Curve

Deer Mountain
10,013 ft

Pierson Mtn.
9,843 ft

Rams Horn Mtn.
9,553 ft

Twin Sisters Peaks
11,428 ft

Pagoda Mtn.
13,497 ft

Chiefs Head Peak
13,579 ft

Gianttrack Mtn.
9,091 ft

Lily Mountain
9,786 ft

Estes Cone
11,006 ft

Longs Peak
14,255 ft

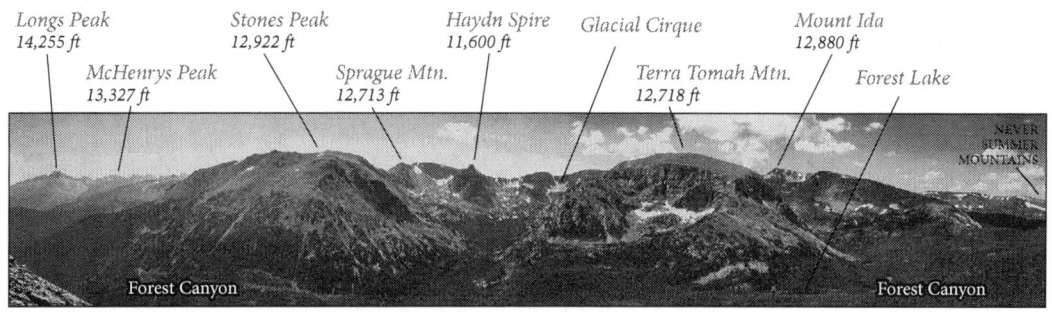

North Lateral Moraine

South Lateral Moraine

Southeast view from the east side of Many Parks Curve

Longs Peak
14,255 ft

Stones Peak
12,922 ft

Haydn Spire
11,600 ft

Glacial Cirque

Mount Ida
12,880 ft

McHenrys Peak
13,327 ft

Sprague Mtn.
12,713 ft

Terra Tomah Mtn.
12,718 ft

Forest Lake

NEVER
SUMMER
MOUNTAINS

Forest Canyon

Forest Canyon

View from Forest Canyon Overlook

Marmot Point
11,909 ft

Mount Chiquita
13,069 ft

Mount Chapin
12,454 ft

Deer Mountain
10,013 ft

Sundance Mountain
12,466 ft

MUMMY RANGE

TRAIL RIDGE

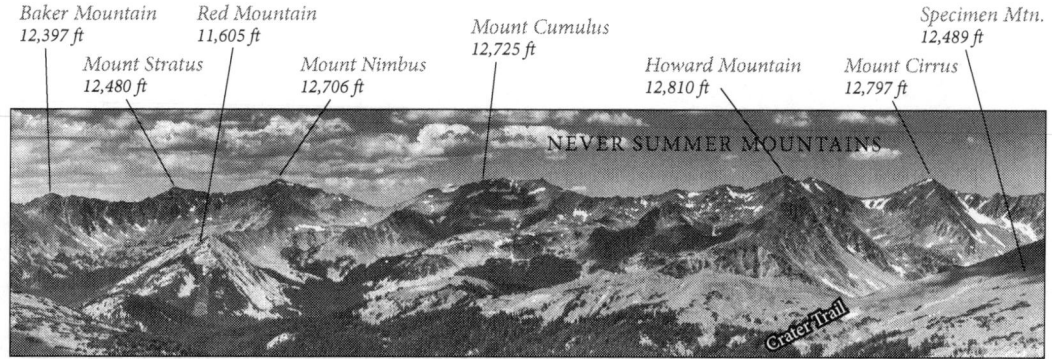

Old Fall River Road

East view from Alpine Visitor Center

Baker Mountain
12,397 ft

Red Mountain
11,605 ft

Mount Cumulus
12,725 ft

Specimen Mtn.
12,489 ft

Mount Stratus
12,480 ft

Mount Nimbus
12,706 ft

Howard Mountain
12,810 ft

Mount Cirrus
12,797 ft

NEVER SUMMER MOUNTAINS

Crater Trail

Never Summer Range seen from Gore Range Overlook

RECOMMENDATIONS

There are many great activities to pursue in Rocky Mountain National Park. But your time is likely limited. Here are our recommendations to get the most out of the park, when you're staying just one or a few days. This will help you to catch the spirit of the park. If you have time, throw in a hike or a picnic, but be warned: time flies in the park!

One day

Part 1: Start at the Fall River Entrance Station. Stop at Sheep Lakes to look out for bighorn sheep. After that enjoy the West Horseshoe Park Overlook.

Part 2: Travel along Bear Lake Road all the way up to Bear Lake. Take the shuttle bus, if you can't find a free parking lot. Admire Bear Lake by taking at least the first 200 yards or the round trip if you feel like it. Go back to your car and leave the Bear Lake region. If you need a breakfast we recommend to stop at Sprague Lake for a self-served picnic.

Part 3: Head straight to the Trail Ridge Road. Stop at Many Parks Curve and Rainbow Curve. At Rock Cut hop out of the car and look for pikas on the downhill side. Head on to the Lava Cliffs. Then refresh yourself at the Alpine Visitor Center and dare to take the strenuous hike up to the Alpine Ridge. Continue a few yards to Medicine Bow Curve, enjoy the vista and turn around. Head back on Trail Ridge Road towards Estes Park and adore the sunset at Gore Range Overlook or Forest Canyon Overlook.

Alternative Route: In case the Old Fall River Road is open, take it up to the Alpine Visitor Center instead of part 3. Stop after 1.4 miles to see the Chasm Falls. Head on to the Alpine Visitor Center and continue as described in part 3.

Two days

Day 1: Explore the Bear Lake Region. Go directly to Bear Lake, have a look at it or circle it, then head on to Nymph Lake and Dream Lake. If you are up to more hiking, take the loop via Lake Haiyaha and Alberta Falls to the Glacier Gorge Trailhead. There you can take the shuttle bus back to your car. The hike sums up to 6.5 miles. Else turn around at Dream Lake and hike back to Bear Lake, covering 2.2 miles total. You could then stop at the Glacier Gorge Trailhead and add 1.6 miles by hiking to the Alberta Falls and back, if you get a parking space. If there is time left, hike or rest at Sprague Lake.

Day 2: Start at the Fall River Entrance Station. Stop at Sheep Lakes to look out for bighorn sheep. After that enjoy the West Horseshoe Park Overlook. Drive the entire Trail Ridge Road (or use the alternative described above on the way up), stopping at Many Parks Curve, Rainbow Curve, Rock Cut (just for the pikas) and Lava Cliffs. Refresh at the Alpine Visitor Center. Head on to Medicine Bow Curve and drive straight to the Coyote Valley Trail. At dusk watch for moose in the Kawuneeche Valley. On your way back embrace the sunset at Gore Range or Forest Canyon Overlook before you return to your accommodation.

Three days

Day 1: Explore the Bear Lake Region as described for the two day tour.

Day 2: Start at the Fall River Entrance Station. Stop at Sheep Lakes to look out for bighorn sheep. After that enjoy the West Horseshoe Park Overlook. Explore the East Trail Ridge Road as described in part 3 of the one day tour. Include Hidden Valley, Rock Cut Community Trail and Alpine Ridge Trail (or Medicine Bow Curve Trail if you want to take it easy). Glory in the setting sun on your way back by watching the sunset from Gore Range or Forest Canyon Overlook. If you're fast and the sun isn't setting yet, go to Moraine Park and watch elk.

Day 3: Explore West Trail Ridge Road. Drive without stop all the way from Estes Park to Medicine Bow Curve. If the Old Fall River Road is open, take this route if you dare and stop at Chasm Falls after 1.4 miles. From Medicine Bow Curve enjoy driving down the western part of Trail Ridge Road. Include all stops down to Harbison Meadows. Hike at Lake Irene, Coyote Valley Trail and perhaps Holzwarth Ranch, watching out for moose. As an alternative hike to Adams Falls. Enjoy the setting sun on your way back.

More than three days

Start with the recommended three day tour. After that the whole park is your playground. In addition to the easier hikes, we recommend you buy one of the hiking guide books at a visitor center, which lead you deeper into the park. Don't miss Bierstadt Lake!

Starting from Grand Lake

The routes described start at Estes Park. To modify them when starting in Grand Lake, please reverse the order of the points of interest. E.g. for a one day trip drive straight to Medicine Bow Curve and enjoy half of the overlooks from there down to Deer Ridge Junction. Then visit Bear Lake and enjoy the setting sun on your way back on Trail Ridge Road. Stop at overlooks that you skipped on the forward run. Or if you dare and the sun is still up, take the alternative route via the Old Fall River Road.

Don't Miss Spots

If you have seen these places, you know what the park is about:

➤ West Horseshoe Park — Because of the view of the Mummy Range
➤ Moraine Park — Because of the Big Thompson River wetlands and the elk

➤ Bear Lake — Because it's the prototype of a Rocky Mountain National Park lake
➤ Dream Lake — Because it's the most beautiful lake that can be reached easily
➤ Alberta Falls — Because they are beautiful falls
➤ Bierstadt Lake — Because of the fabulous calm and quiet vista and the moraine

➤ Rainbow Curve — Because of the view of Horseshoe Park
➤ Forest Canyon Overlook — Because of the view and the magnificent sunset
➤ Gore Range Overlook — Because of the mountain view and the delightful sunset
➤ Alpine Visitor Center — Because of the glacial cirque and the restrooms
➤ Alpine Ridge Trail — Because of the magnificent 360° viewing

➤ Lake Irene — Because of the beautiful, quiet lake
➤ Coyote Valley Trail — Because of the Kawuneeche Valley and the Colorado River
➤ Kawuneeche Valley — Because of the moose

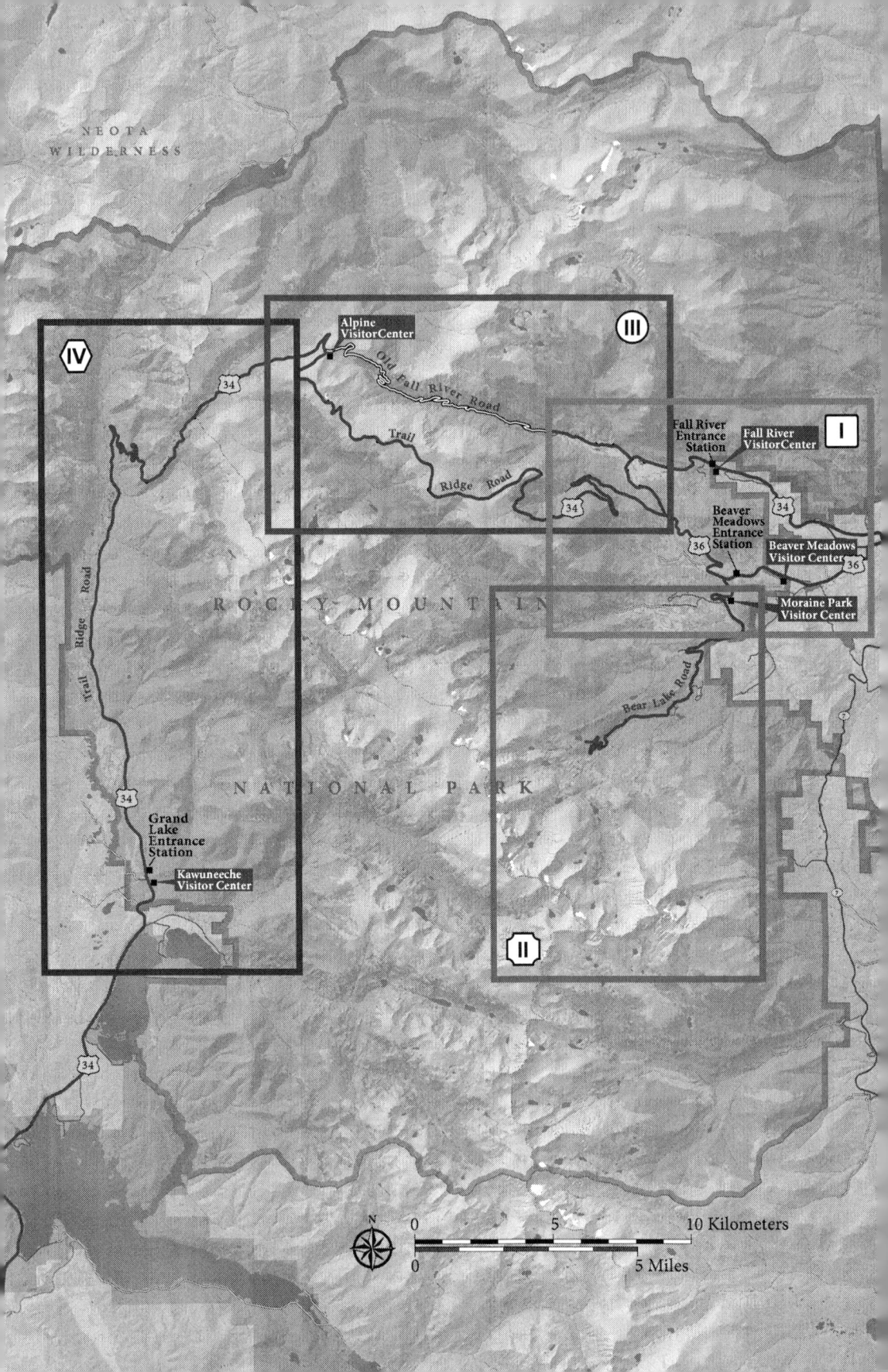

REGIONS OVERVIEW

The map on the left gives you an overview of the park and the different regions we recommend you visit. At the park entrance you will receive a more detailed map from the park rangers. You can also download this map as a PDF file from the park's website or via a link from our homepage.

I   Horseshoe and Moraine Park

The Horseshoe and Moraine Park region is characterized by it's beautiful meadows and wetlands. Wildlife watching, picnicking or just hanging out and embracing nature are the main activities here. Nonetheless the avid hiker can find many trails leading up high into the mountains and the wildlife watcher might see elk and even bighorn sheep.

II   Bear Lake Region

The Bear Lake Region is the most visited region of the park. It offers a great combination of lakes, waterfalls and scenic backdrops. Even if you only got one day in the park, you shouldn't omit the Bear Lake region. It's also *the* place to hike in the park.

III   East Trail Ridge Road

This section starts at Deer Ridge Junction and leads from montane forests up into the alpine tundra. The main draws here are great views of the mountain scenery and insights into the park's geology. And don't forget to enjoy the tiny beauty of what grows and crawls in the alpine tundra.

IV   West Trail Ridge Road

Not as heavily visited as the east side of the park, the western part offers great hikes, e.g. along the young Colorado River, to the Never Summer Mountain Range or to distant lakes. It also gives you plenty opportunities for watching wildlife. Especially moose, elk and mule deer can be found here.

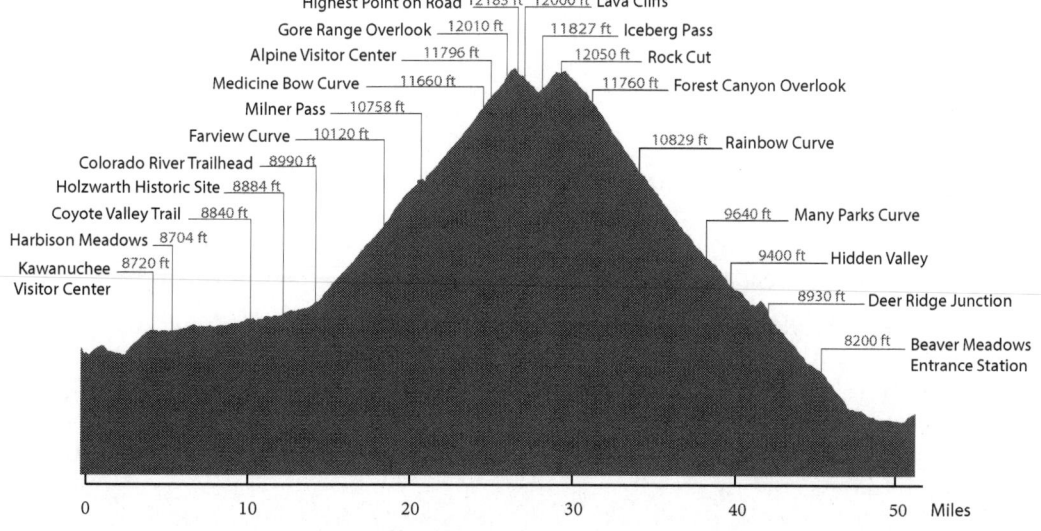

Elevation profile of Trail Ridge Road from west to east

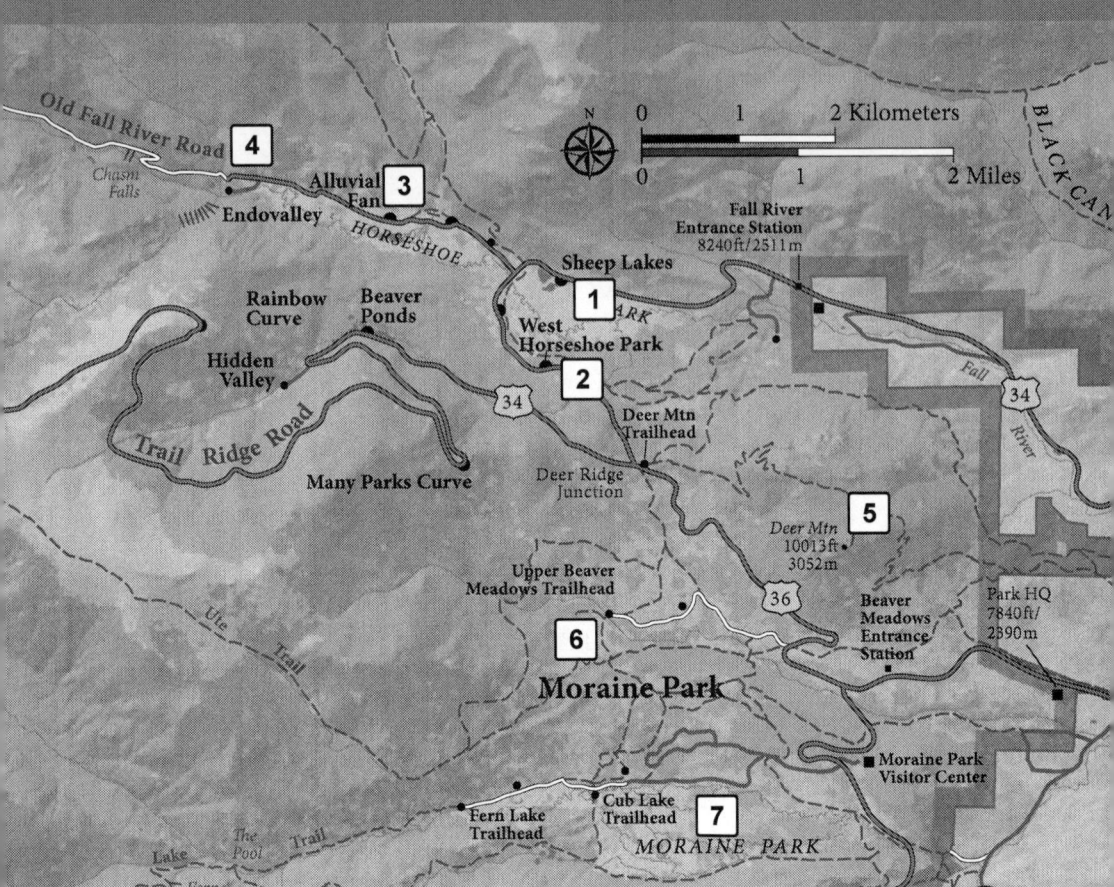

HORSESHOE PARK & MORAINE PARK

The landscape of this region is made up of valleys surrounded by mountains. These valleys are called "parks" in Colorado. Hence the town name Estes Park, because it is located in a similar setting. The valleys in Moraine Park were created by glaciers. They are covered by lush meadows and surrounded by forests, growing on moraines. Beyond that, beautiful alpine peaks form the background. It's a place for animals to graze and visitors to relax. You can walk the meadows freely or follow one of the many trails.

Horseshoe Park is the first of the three big meadows that comprise this region. It got its name from the early settlers who thought the meandering Fall River looked like horseshoes. Eighty years ago the meadows were used as a big campground for workers of the Civilian Conservation Corps who built many roads and trails in the park during the Great Depression. Today nature has reclaimed the meadows, leaving no trace. This place looks best in the morning, when the Mummy Range is lit by the rising sun.

The second big meadow is Beaver Meadows. It is the most remote and quiet of the three, because it is not directly adjacent to one of the big roads, but can only be reached by a narrow and not maintained road. If you want to enjoy the lower elevations of the park mostly undisturbed, this is the place to go. Moraine Park is the third and biggest of the three meadows. Alongside it runs Fern Lake Road, which is served by the Moraine Park shuttle bus, making it easily accessible.

West Horseshoe Park Overlook

1 Sheep Lakes *8,520 ft*

The Sheep Lakes are named after the bighorn sheep that can be found here from time to time, traveling down from the Mummy Range where they usually graze and dwell. The best chance to see bighorn sheep at Sheep Lakes is from May to June, when the lambing period is over. They don't come for the water but for minerals like sodium, iron, magnesium and zinc, which they find in the soil around the lakes. In the summer the lucky visitor equipped with a good lens might also spot bighorn sheep on the steep and stony cliffs of Bighorn Mountain. You need good eyes to distinguish them from the grayish-brown rocks. The rangers and volunteers have trained eyes and will help you to spot them when they are on duty at Sheep Lakes. They will also stop the traffic when bighorn sheep want to cross the street. You might wonder, why such a big parking lot is needed, but it will quickly fill up, when sheep are around.

2 West Horseshoe Park *8,734 ft*

Don't miss the West Horseshoe Park Overlook half-way between Sheep Lakes and Deer Ridge Junction. It gives you a great view over the Sheep Lakes area and, weather permitting, an exceptional look at the treeless peaks of the Mummy Range — Mount Chapin, Mount Chiquita, Ypsilon Mountain and Fairchild Mountain — and the Alluvial Fan in front of them. In the foreground you will see the Fall River meandering through the lush meadows of Horseshoe Park. The nearby trees offer shelter and food to hummingbirds, crossbills, magpies and other birds.

Bighorn sheep at Sheep Lakes

3 | Alluvial Fan *8,610 ft*

A deposition of rocks and sediment by a creek, forming the shape of a fan or cone, is called an alluvial fan. It typically can be found where a narrow canyon in the mountains widens into a field. The Alluvial Fan in Rocky Mountain National Park gives tribute to the mighty geological forces shaping the world. Water shaped the entire park and the Alluvial Fan is a place where you still can see that happening. 1982 on the 15th of July, the Lawn Lake waters broke through a moraine, wreaking havoc. Water, mud and huge boulders were spilled downhill and created the Alluvial Fan. The 2013 flood, caused by intense rain, reshaped the Alluvial Fan to it's current extent. The street and bridge leading over the creek were swept away by the rushing water and the parking lot for visitors was covered by large boulders. The park rangers just finished repairing the road in October 2014 and are currently still working on restoring the park-

The Alluvial Fan before .....

... and after the flood in 2013

ing lot. The Alluvial Fan lies at the entrance to the Old Fall River Road, which is the predecessor of the Trail Ridge Road and an alternative one-way route up to the Alpine Visitor Center.

Great horned owl hatchling in the forest east of the Alluvial Fan

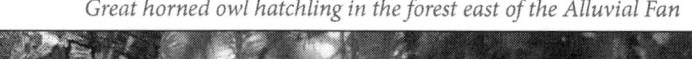

Left: Fall River close to the Alluvial Fan. Sundance Mountain to the left and Mount Chapin to the right.

4 | Old Fall River Road *8,558 - 11,796 ft*

Before the well maintained Trail Ridge Road with its many overlooks was built, the Alpine Visitor Center up in the treeless alpine tundra was already there. It could be reached by the Fall River Road, which is nowadays called the Old Fall River Road. Completed in 1920 it is a much more demanding and adventurous drive and an experience of its own. The Old Fall River Road starts in the curve at Horseshoe Park, close to the Sheep Lakes. It takes you past the Alluvial Fan up the mountainside of Mount Chapin, always following the Fall River. The narrow dirt road with tight curves is 9 miles long and offers steep grades up to 16%. Long vehicles (24 ft+) are not allowed. Because it is so narrow and has only a few pullouts, it nowadays is a one-way road. The road leads you right along the mountainside through beautiful forests. It feels like a hiking trail for cars and is very scenic. Since you're only allowed to go 15 mph and should take frequent stops to enjoy the scenery, the journey will take an hour or more.

If you're planning a round trip of the entire Trail Ridge Road or just going up to the Alpine Visitor Center and you and your car feel you're up to the challenge, you can take the Old Fall River Road on the way up instead of the Trail Ridge Road. This way, you get to see and use both roads in one trip. When you take the Old Fall River Road don't forget to stop at the Chasm Falls located just a mile after the gravel part of the road starts. These 25 feet high waterfalls, which created beautiful potholes over time, are easily accessible by a short trail but can be overlooked if you don't watch out for them.

Unfortunately the Old Fall River Road was heavily damaged by the flood in 2013 and has stayed closed since then. However, the National Park Service is working to repair it and expects to re-open it on the Fourth of July weekend 2015. Please check the park's website for details or changes as this date approaches. When the road is re-opened, it will be accessible only during summer and close at first snowfall.

Old Fall River Road

5 Deer Mountain *10,013 ft*

Deer Mountain is not one of the highest mountains, but due to its exposed location in Horseshoe Park it provides the humble hiker with exceptional views of the surrounding mountains including the prominent Mummy Range to the north and Longs Peak to the south. Deer Mountain itself is densely wooded but there are enough overlooks to make it well worth to do the hike. Because Deer Mountain stands isolated, it receives plenty of sunshine, making the trail up the mountain one of the first hikes to become snow-free in late spring and it usually stays like this until early winter.

Deer Mountain

The hike itself is 6 miles long as a round trip and the trail is well maintained. With more than 1,000 feet elevation gain it is rather steep, requiring some physical fitness, especially when you're not yet well adjusted to the altitude of about 10,000 feet. The first overlook facing Longs Peak can be reached after just a few hundred yards. After almost a mile, the first great view towards the Mummy Range with the prominent peaks Chapin, Chiquita and Ypsilon is granted. After two miles the trail levels, while you hike along the ridge top. After another half mile it starts going down a bit and up again before it becomes steep while you climb the last few hundred feet to the summit. The Deer Mountain summit offers a great view over 360 degrees, showing you most of the eastern half of the park up to the Continental Divide. You also have an unblemished view of Estes Park.

View south from Deer Mountain shortly before sunset

6 Upper Beaver Meadows *8,290 ft*

If you're looking for lush meadows and wildflowers, the montane ecosystem of the Upper Beaver Meadows might be just right for you. And if that's not enough there are trees and the occasional elk as well. The area can be reached by an unmaintained road that goes off from U.S. Highway 36 about a mile after the Bear Lake Road junction. The small road runs for 1.6 miles to the Upper Beaver Meadows Trailhead, but you can also stop and wander around in the meadows at different points before that. During the winter months the road leading to the Upper Beaver Meadows is closed to cars and becomes a hiking trail by itself.

Upper Beaver Meadows

The trailhead has, unlike other trailheads, not just one trail to hike, but several directions to head off to. You can even access the Ute Trail from here that leads all the way up to the continental divide. Hiking in the Upper Beaver Meadows is relaxed and on many days you will be pretty much to yourself. It's a great place to inhale the peace and beauty of nature. You may also enter the fenced areas, but make sure to close the gates behind you. They are set up to keep elk out, not people. You may notice that the vegetation grows very well inside the fence without the elk feeding on the saplings.

7 Moraine Park *8,081 ft*

Moraine Park is a valley formed by a glacier and surrounded by moraines, easily recognizable as rolling hills. They are covered with ponderosa pines on the dryer south-facing slopes and lodgepole pines, Douglas fir and ponderosa pines on the more humid north-facing slopes. The valley is an ideal place for elks to graze and people to stroll. Moraine Park is located at Bear Lake Road across from the visitor center bearing the same name. It sports many trails, some just to wander around in the meadows, others to reach destinations beyond that, like Cub Lake and The Pool. The Big Thompson River flows gently through the meadows. On its northern side runs Fern Lake Road, leading to the Fern Lake Trailhead, which is also a shuttle bus stop. The woods on the northern lateral moraine host the Moraine Park Campground.

The easiest way to enjoy Moraine Park is to park the car at one of the many parking lots along Fern Lake Road and just wander along the road and into the meadows. For a longer hike one can start at the Cub Lake Trailhead, but turn left — instead of right towards Cub Lake — after half a mile and hike towards Bear Lake Road. From there the trail leads north along the road. When the trail heads back into the meadow you can either continue to follow it, reaching Fern Lake Road after a while, which leads you back towards your start. Or you take the shuttle bus at Moraine Park Visitor Center back to the Cub Lake Trailhead.

Moraine Park is also the premiere area in the park to watch the elk rut in September. Starting at 5 p.m. the meadows then will be closed for visitors. Simply park your car at the curb of Fern Lake Road and follow the crowd. Usually the elk can be spotted easily from the roadside.

Left: Sunset at Moraine Park. Elk can been seen grazing in the valley every evening.

BEAR LAKE REGION

The Bear Lake Region impresses with wild creeks, stunning waterfalls and pristine lakes, all in front of majestic peaks. Especially the flat-topped Longs Peak is easily recognizable by its unique shape and the jagged crest. To the right of Longs Peak, the eastern side of the Continental Divide is formed by the steep north face of Hallett Peak and Flattop Mountain, which doesn't look all that flat from down below. The valley between the two peaks contains Tyndall Glacier.

The Bear Lake Region is the premier hiking region in Rocky Mountain National Park. Many short and long, level and steep, easy and difficult trails can be found here, providing something for every hiker. The main destinations are the lakes of the region, usually set in front of one or more peaks. On the following pages we will present some of those lakes for you to chose from, if you plan to hike in the park.

Little falls everywhere

Access to the region is provided by the Bear Lake Road, which exits U.S. Highway 36 after the Beaver Meadows Entrance Station. It winds its way up the mountains toward the southwest for 10 miles, climbing from 8,200 feet to about 9,400 feet at Bear Lake. In contrast to Trail Ridge Road, which closes during the winter, Bear Lake Road stays open year round. If you plan to park at Bear Lake or a trailhead close to it, you should arrive early, because the lots usually fill up quickly in the morning. Alternatively the shuttle bus will get you there from the large Park & Ride area located half way down the Bear Lake Road.

Hallett Peak (left) and Flattop Mountain can be seen from the Bear Lake parking lot, which fills fast in the morning

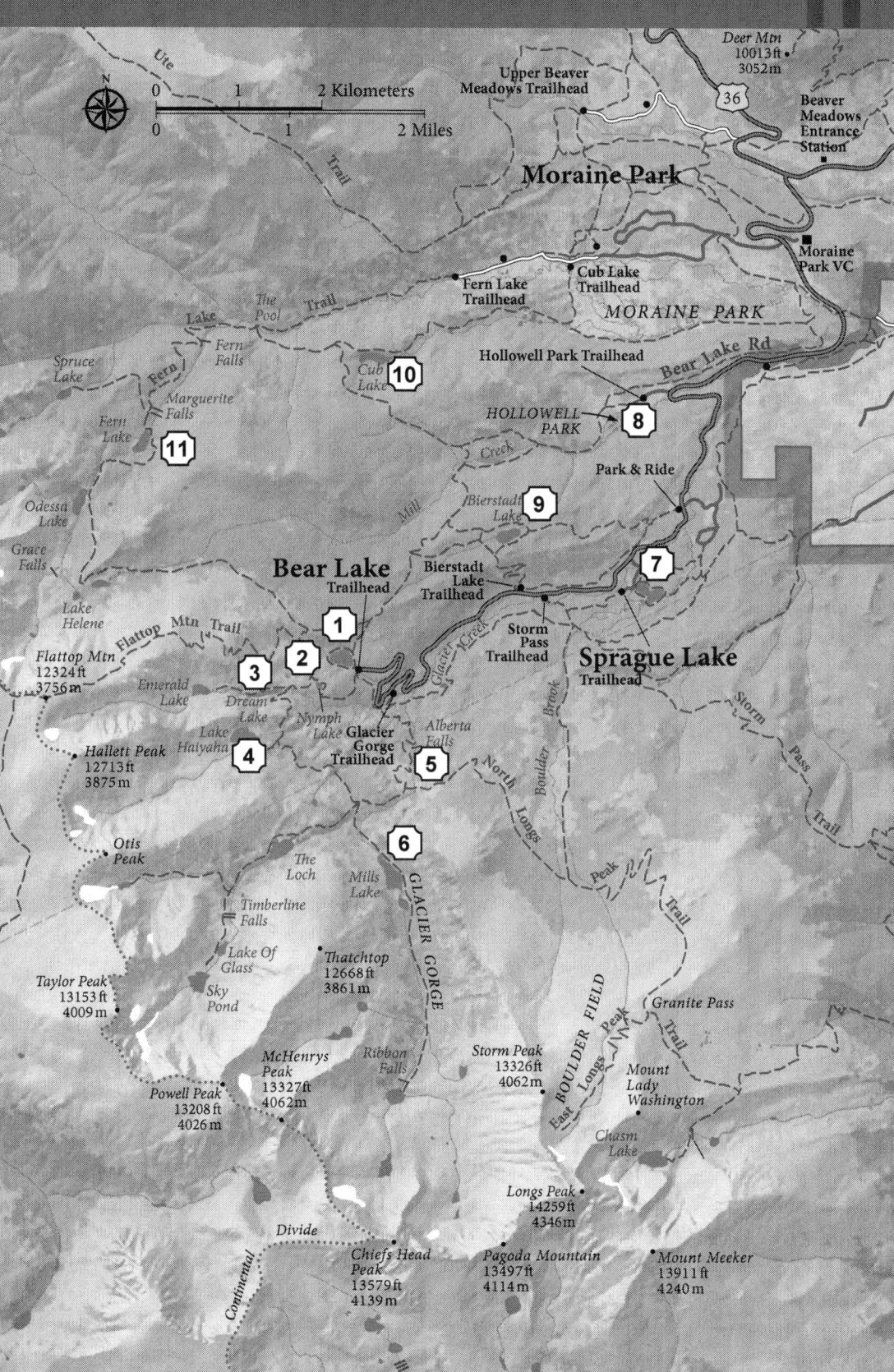

With it's fabulous backdrop and the good accessibility Bear Lake is a must see

[1] Bear Lake *9,475 ft*

Bear Lake is reached on Bear Lake Road by car or shuttle bus. This marvelous lake is visited by many people, because it is easy to reach, extraordinary beautiful and a starting point for many far-reaching trails. Bear Lake lies at the base of Hallett Peak and Flattop Mountain, giving it a beautiful alpine background right at the beginning of the trail. Reaching the northern part of the lake, the impressive Longs Peak takes over when you look to the south.

This gives the visitor another reason to come early in the morning. Not only do you avoid the larger crowds, but also the peaks will be reflected in the lake. If you're only planning a short hike, you can also come in the late afternoon for an emptier parking lot. The trail around the lake is half a mile short and easy to hike. It's well maintained and has a self-guided interpretive tour going counter-clockwise. It is not paved, but has a hard packed surface making it partly wheelchair accessible, when the ground is dry.

[2] Nymph Lake *9,700 ft*

To the left of Bear Lake Trailhead the trails to Nymph Lake, Dream Lake, Lake Haiyaha and some other lakes can be found. Nymph Lake is closest by, only half a mile from the trailhead. The trail gains 225 feet in elevation over the short distance. But since it's so short, it still makes a good trail for families even with small children.

The small natural lake is surrounded by Hallett Peak and Longs Peak and covered by many pond lilies, blossoming during the summer. Occasionally ducks can be seen swimming on the lake and colorful dragonflies catch your eyes with their large multi-faceted eyes, two pairs of strong, transparent wings, and an elongated body. After you stayed and enjoyed the lake you can head on to Dream Lake or back to Bear Lake.

Right: Pond lilies embellish Nymph Lake

Hallett Peak and Flattop Mountain are steady companions on your way to Dream Lake

[3] Dream Lake *9,900 ft*

After hiking to Nymph Lake you can continue on the same trail, reaching Dream Lake after 0.6 miles. The path leads through pine forests and continues to gain in altitude, clearing another 200 feet before you reach your destination. The last part of the trail consists of switchbacks, leading you along the wild Tyndall Creek.

Dream Lake is one of the most beautiful lakes in the Bear Lake Region. Hallett Peak and Flattop Mountain form the silhouette behind the lake, making for some great pictures. A peninsula on the northern side, where the trail arrives, makes for a great place to rest and perhaps eat lunch. Continuing from Dream Lake you can either go west to Emerald Lake or walk a few feet back and turn south towards Lake Haiyaha.

[4] Lake Haiyaha *10,220 ft*

The hike to Lake Haiyaha from Dream Lake takes you through the subalpine forest for another mile, gaining over 300 feet in altitude. Before you reach the lake, you have to cross some rugged terrain on the last hundred yards, made up of many impressive boulders, left by the glacier that formed this landscape. Lake Haiyaha is lined by Hallett Peak and Otis Peak. The small glacier between the two peaks feeds the lake and Chaos Creek, which emerges from the lake and gives the Chaos Canyon it's name. If you take a look back, you will also be able to see the Mummy Range far away in the northern part of the park.

From Lake Haiyaha you can either turn around and go back towards Bear Lake or go on to Mills Lake almost three miles away. If you want to enjoy other places in the park on that day, we suggest you turn around here.

Right: Lake Haiyaha at the bottom of Hallett Peak

Mills Lake with Longs Peak, Pagoda Mountain and Chief' Head Peak in the background

5 Mills Lake *9,940 ft*

Mills Lake can be reached by continuing 2.7 miles after Lake Haiyaha or 2 miles from the Alberta Falls (see below). This beautiful subalpine lake is surrounded by impressive mountain tops. It lies at the foot of Half Mountain. To the south you can spot Longs Peak, Pagoda Mountain, Chiefs Head Peak and Thatchtop. Many logs fill the lake, taking hundreds of years to decay. The water is crystal clear, which is loved by hikers and anglers as well. The lake was named after Enos Mills, the driving force behind the creation of Rocky Mountain National Park. Take the time and hike just past Mills Lake. You will find a marvelous appendix called Jewel Lake.

6 Alberta Falls *9,400 ft*

Although the Alberta Falls can be reached from Lake Haiyaha, the by far shorter way to the falls starts at the Glacier Gorge Trailhead, which lies one shuttle bus stop before Bear Lake. Going there by car is usually not advisable, because the small parking lot is filled up in early morning.

The path follows Glacier Creek for 0.8 miles. About half the way you reach a prolonged intersection, where the crossing trail shares a bit of the way with your trail. This other trail takes you, depending on the direction, to either Bear Lake or Sprague Lake. Continuing you will soon hear the falls. After a sharp curve you will finally see the Alberta Falls, which are among the most beautiful in the park.

Alberta Falls in June

Sprague Lake with Estes Cone to the right

7 Sprague Lake *8,710 ft*

En route to Bear Lake you pass a small turnoff that brings you to Sprague Lake after a quarter mile. The lake has a fairly large parking lot and a trail that leads in a loop around the lake. The trail is made of packed gravel and wheelchair accessible. Along the way you will find benches to rest as well as platforms for fishing. The level round-trip is a little less than a mile long and designed as an interpretive trail. The lake is a great location for photographers, especially when they arrive early. At sunrise the glowing mountains of the Continental Divide are mirrored in the calm lake and the light is good for reflections all morning long. The lake is named after Abner Sprague, who owned a resort at the lake before Rocky Mountain National Park was designated in 1915.

8 Hollowell Park *8,300 ft*

Hollowell Park may not be as spectacular as some other places, but it serves as a quiet oasis in the otherwise quite busy Bear Lake Region. Back in the 1930s the Civilian Conservation Corps, which built many structures in the park, had two cabins here. Today there is a nice picnic area instead. Close to the trailhead the Mill Creek created a beautiful wetland with trouts racing in the small streams. In the distance a light green trail on the Bierstadt Moraine marks old logging activities from a time before the park was created.

Hollowell Park Trail

9 Bierstadt Lake *9,416 ft*

Bierstadt Lake is truly a gem you shouldn't miss, if your time in the park permits the hike. There are several ways to reach the lake. The easiest is to take the 2 mile trail from Bear Lake, because you start at a higher altitude. It branches off the Bear Lake Trail on

the eastern side of the lake a few hundred feet after the trailhead. At first it goes uphill, but once you pass the intersection with the Fern Lake Trail it's almost completely down-hill. When you come close to Bierstadt Lake, watch for a sign saying 'trail around lake' and take that route.

The lake is extremely beautiful from all sides. Arguably the best view is from the eastern end towards the Continental Divide with Hallett Peak and Flattop Mountain in the background. When you're done adoring the lake you have three options to continue: go to the Park & Ride area, continue your

View from the Bierstadt moraine

hike towards Cub Lake or go to the Bierstadt Trailhead, which we recommend. This hike takes you straight down the Bierstadt Moraine with yaw-dropping views of the Continental Divide and the surrounding forests, especially in the fall. But watch the clock if you have to take the shuttle bus, because admiring all the beauty lets time fly and the last bus to the Park & Ride area usually leaves around 7:00 p.m.

The beautiful sky and backdrop are mirrored in Bierstadt Lake

10 Cub Lake *8,620 ft*

The Cub Lake Trailhead is located on Fern Lake Road and can be reached by car and shuttle bus. The 2.3 miles long trail takes you through the Moraine Park meadow before it becomes much steeper, climbing along a wooded hillside for a gain of about 550 feet in altitude. As you hike along the trail you will see signs of the 2012 Fern Lake Fire. An illegal campfire in the Forest Canyon went loose and burned down nearly 3,500 acres of forest and meadow land, making it the worst fire in the park's history. This high altitude winter fire affected wildlife as well as visitors. Its scars will be visible for a long time. Nonetheless the trail to Cub Lake and the lake itself are well worth the hike. Nature is restoring and green is making a comeback. Especially in the evening, when the sun illuminates Cub Lake with an orange color and the burned mountain sides lie in the shadows, hikers can embrace the silent beauty of this pond lily covered lake. Don't forget to take a deep look into the water to see different kinds of fish scurrying back and forth in search for food and shelter.

Cub Lake

The Pool

11 Fern Lake *9,530 ft*

One that sets out for Fern Lake shouldn't have other plans for the day. The hike is both long and strenuous, no matter from which of the two possible ends you start. The recommended but slightly longer option is to start at Bear Lake and hike all the way to the Fern Lake Trailhead, making it a 9 mile trip. As an added benefit when starting at Bear Lake, you will pass Lake Helene and Odessa Lake with some fantastic mountain views along the way. After a rather steep first quarter it's mostly downhill. Behind Fern Lake you continue downwards to the Fern Lake Trailhead near Moraine Park, passing Fern Falls and The Pool on the way. From there you can take the shuttle bus back to Bear Lake, switching buses at the Park & Ride area.

Fern Falls

If you start at Fern Lake Trailhead, you should consider turning around at Fern Lake, instead of climbing all the way to Bear Lake. The hike to Fern Lake is already steep, gaining 1,400 feet. Returning to the trailhead makes it an eight mile round-trip.

Fern Lake

EAST TRAIL RIDGE ROAD

Starting from Deer Ridge Junction near Horseshoe Park the Trail Ridge Road, also known as U.S. Highway 34, leads you up into the alpine parts of Rocky Mountain National Park. Beyond the high altitude lands, it continues through the western part of the park to the town of Grand Lake. From mid-October to Memorial Day the road is closed between the Many Parks Curve in the east and Timberlake Trailhead in the west. For this book we have divided Trail Ridge Road into an eastern and a western part. The cutoff is the Medicine Bow Curve, located right after the Alpine Visitor Center.

The road starts in the low-lying meadow-lands of the park, which include small treasures like Beaver Ponds and Hidden Valley. Starting to climb to higher elevations, it displays some of the most scenic vistas in the park, especially Rainbow Curve and Forest Canyon Overlook. At about 11,500 feet you reach the treeline and enter a completely new ecosystem: the alpine tundra, where pikas, marmots and bighorn sheep dwell and big herds of elk graze. Trail Ridge Road is the highest continuously paved highway in the entire nation with several spectacular overlooks in the high country. It peaks at 12,183 feet shortly after the Lava Cliffs Overlook. One stop before that, at Rock Cut, the Tundra Communities Trail brings you up to about the same altitude. The short one mile out and back hike leads upwards past some large funny shaped rocks, called mushroom rocks, to a great view of the alpine peaks.

Trail Ridge Road continues on to the Alpine Visitor Center. On the other side of the parking lot, the Old Fall River Road comes up the mountain. The view down the old road on the backside of the visitor center displays a breathtaking alpine scenery. If you're short on time, you can use the visitor center or Medicine Bow Curve just beyond it to turn around. If you enjoy scenic views, you can take the short trail on the right side of Medicine Bow Curve, leading you around the mountain.

Bull elk gathering cows in the alpine tundra during the rut

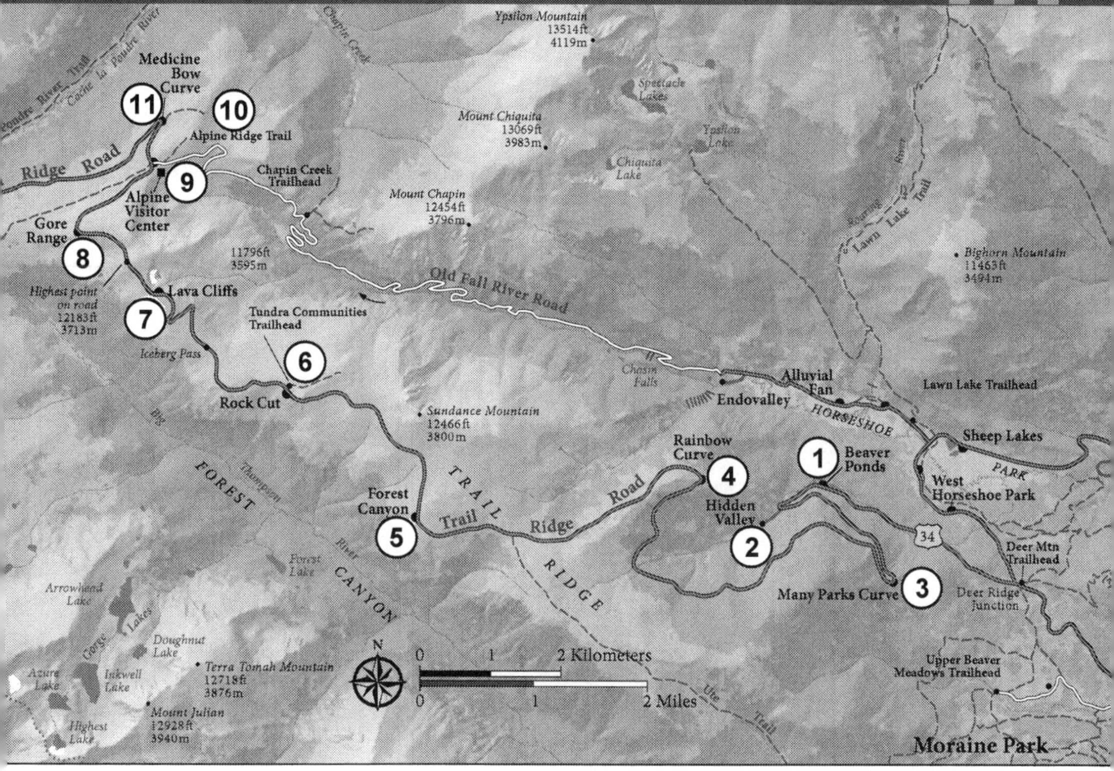
Ypsilon Mountain
13514ft
4119m
Medicine
Bow
Curve
11
10
Alpine Ridge Trail
Ridge Road
Spectacle
Lakes
Mount Chiquita
13069ft
3983m
Ypsilon
Lake
Chiquita
Lake
Chapin Creek
Trailhead
9
Alpine
Visitor
Center
Mount Chapin
12454ft
3796m
Gore
Range
8
11796ft
3595m
Bighorn Mountain
11463ft
3494m
Lawn Lake Trail
Old Fall River Road
Lava Cliffs
Highest point
on road
12183ft
3713m
7
Tundra Communities
Trailhead
Iceberg Pass
6
Rock Cut
Chasm
Falls
Alluvial
Fan
Endovalley
Lawn Lake Trailhead
HORSESHOE
PARK
Sundance Mountain
12466ft
3800m
Rainbow
Curve
4
1
Beaver
Ponds
Sheep Lakes
West
Horseshoe Park
FOREST
CANYON
Forest
Canyon
5
TRAIL
RIDGE
Trail Ridge Road
Hidden
Valley
2
34
Deer Mtn
Trailhead
Many Parks Curve
3
Deer Ridge
Junction
Arrowhead
Lake
Forest
Lake
Doughnut
Lake
Azure
Lake
Inkwell
Lake
Terra Tomah Mountain
12718ft
3876m
N
0
1
2 Kilometers
0
1
2 Miles
Mount Julian
12928ft
3940m
Highest
Lake
Ute Trail
Upper Beaver
Meadows Trailhead
Moraine Park

① Beaver Ponds *9,004 ft*

The Beaver Ponds are a small, but idyllic location. Their name is easy to confuse with the picnic area carrying the same name on the west side of Trail Ridge Road. The Beaver Ponds were created, when the Hidden Valley Creek was dammed by beavers, forming a large pond. Over time the dam decayed and the water of the pond was drained, exposing very fertile soil that was collected at the bottom of the pond. This soil was the starter for a lush meadow, forming a great habitat for insects, salamander, birds and elk. The meadow later will give way to a growing forest — unless the beavers rebuild the dam and renew the cycle. The Beaver Ponds in their current state can be visited on a small boardwalk, leading to a platform on top of the creek. It's a great place to relax and also a nice place to fish. However, due to the reintroduction of the endangered native greenback cutthroat trout, a strict catch and release policy for these fish is in place.

Beaver Ponds seen from Rainbow Curve

Visitors at the Beaver Ponds platform

(2) Hidden Valley *9,240 ft*

Parking lot and picnic area

Ancient forest of Hidden Valley

Hidden Valley had many uses over time. At first, back in the late 1800s, parts of the forest were logged and a saw mill operated there. Later it became a ski area that operated until 1992. The buildings were then deconstructed and the materials reused to build other structures all over the park. Ever since it has been what it is now: a lush and scenic place in the park, ideal for a picnic or a short hike along the Hidden Valley Creek. If you want to learn more about the valley, you can follow the interpretive trail while hiking, which is also a great way to enjoy wildflowers. For picnicking several well maintained tables along the trail can be used. In the winter Hidden Valley offers a fenced-off area where families can enjoy sledding and snow-play. Skiing and snowboarding also guarantee for fun.

Due to the abundance of water in the valley and large amounts of snow piling up in the winter, the forest in Hidden Valley has in most parts been spared from forest fires for hundreds of years. Thus many trees are 600 years and older, giving shelter to rare birds and offering shade for the only place in Colorado where feather moss can be found.

(3) Many Parks Curve *9,640 ft*

Many Parks Curve is the first major overlook on Trail Ridge Road. You can park at the beginning or at the end of the curve. The curve presents you a great panoramic and

Great views from Many Parks Curve

scenic view. It is called Many Parks Curve because you can see many of the meadows in the east side of the park. These open areas enclosed by mountains are called parks in the Colorado mountains. If you climb the rocks on the lower end of the curve, you can also peak into the otherwise hidden Horseshoe Park. The rocks are easy to climb and the expanded view is well worth the effort. The overall view ranges from Horseshoe Park in the north, across Deer Mountain, to the Continental Divide behind the Bear Lake Region in the south.

(4) Rainbow Curve 10,829 ft

Rainbow Curve is a great place to take a look at Horseshoe Park from above. To the left you can spot the Alluvial Fan and below it you can find the Fall River meandering through the valley. Further down the Sheep Lakes are shining in dark blue in the middle of Horseshoe Park. Deer Mountain in the center blocks the sight of Estes Park, which peeks through to the left and right of the mountain. Looking down in front of Deer Mountain and close to the road you can also determine where the Beaver Ponds are. Perhaps even some visitors with binoculars spot you from the wooden platform there while you're peeking down on them. Rainbow Curve is also one of the best places to watch the sunrise in the park.

Clark's nutcracker looking for food

Many little critters can be found at Rainbow Curve. Golden-mantled squirrels and least chipmunks race along the small curve-wall, cute little pikas bathe in the sun and Clark's nutcracker as well as the beautiful gray jays fly seemingly playful close to the visitors and their cars. They hope for food, accidentally or by purpose dropped by the visitors. Please withstand the almost overwhelming temptation to feed any wildlife, because it harms the animals.

Horseshoe Park, surrounded by Bighorn Mountain, McGregor Mountain and Deer Mountain, as seen from the Rainbow Curve. The Alluvial Fan and the Beaver Ponds can be seen as well.

(5) Forest Canyon Overlook   *11,716 ft*

The vista from this overlook is overwhelming. Facing the Continental Divide, one peak after the other is lined up on the other side of Forest Canyon, which lies below. Even

Longs Peak can be seen in the southeast. Stones Peak and Terra Tomah Mountain dominate the view to the south. Several glacial cirques, birthplaces of glaciers, can be seen and deep forests hide the Big Thompson River down in the valley. The canyon and it's flanking mountain peaks are most impressive when some but not all the snow on the mountaintops has melted, revealing the rugged cliffs. The rocky surroundings of the overlook are also a playground for marmots, pikas and chipmunks.

Stones Peak behind the Forest Canyon

Beneath the overlook lies Forest Canyon. This beautiful valley between the Trail Ridge and the Continental Divide, was formed by the Big Thompson River. Here wildlife is usually undisturbed by humans because the canyon is not easy to access. Steep terrain and fallen trees everywhere make it unpleasant to hike in this old growth forest. Don't get lost there! Rescue missions in Forest Canyon are extremely difficult to perform. The few human beings visiting these woods are usually scientists. They provide the park management with useful information that helps to better understand and protect this subalpine forest habitat.

Due to the many-colored tundra in the foreground and the fabulous skyline, the Forest Canyon Overlook is not only a great place to take pictures during the day, but also a fantastic place for watching and photographing the sunset.

West view into the Forest Canyon

⑥ Rock Cut and Tundra Communities Trail *12,050 ft*

Rock Cut gives you two quite different things on either side of the road. On the one side you can explore the landscape on the Tundra Communities Trail. On the other side, if you look downhill into the scattered rocks, you will likely first hear and then see the adorable pikas. These tiny relatives of rabbits prefer the cold weather above the treeline and many of them are living here, always busy gathering food.

Find the pika!
It's well disguised.

The Tundra Communities Trail is also called "Tundra Trail" or "Toll Memorial Trail". It's a half-mile interpretive trail which invites you to discover the tundra vegetation and wildlife. The difference in elevation is 260 feet, making it rather steep and literally breathtaking at the altitude of 12,000 feet. Along the trail you will see mushroom-shaped rocks. Their stems are granite and the dark caps are made of schist. Signs along the trail will tell you how they were formed. The trail is heavily used by visitors so please do not leave the trail and give the fragile life around it a chance to survive.

Mushroom rocks

It can be quite windy and cold at this altitude, thus giving you a glimpse of the harsh weather conditions to which life in the tundra has to adapt. But there are also opportunities you wouldn't expect. Up to 150 mph strong winds in the winter hinder snow from piling up. This gives bighorn sheep and elk as well as marmots, pikas, birds and other little creatures the chance to feed when other places are already covered by snow. Take a closer look and discover the fascinating communities that form in this treeless part of the park.

Southeast view from the Tundra Communities Trail

The eroded Lava Cliffs

(7) Lava Cliffs *12,000 ft*

The Lava Cliffs consist of welded tuff which is millions of years old and originates from volcanic activities of the Never Summer Mountains in the west. The tuff has been exposed due to long and consistent erosion caused by glacial activities. The cliff is about 300 feet high and offers shelter for several kinds of birds and butterflies. Don't hesitate to walk closer to the cliff to examine it's fantastic geological features. Visit the Lava Cliffs in the morning if you want to take a good picture, else they will lie in their own shadow. The snow that gathers in this shaded area feeds a little lake, the Iceberg Lake, when it melts away slowly during the summer.

(8) Gore Range Overlook *12,010 ft*

This overlook gives you a stunning view of several mountain ranges. Starting with Longs Peak to the far left the sight continues on the other side of Forest Canyon with Stones Peak, Mount Julian, Mount Ida and the Gore Range in the far back. To the right the Never Summer Mountains can be seen, namely Mount Baker, Mount

Nimbus and Howard Mountain among others. The Gore Range Overlook is a great place to photograph Longs Peak and Stones Peak in the evening sun, catching them with Alpenglow at sunset. Also you can catch a colorful sunset behind the Never Summer Mountains silhouette. However, for beautiful pictures of the range itself, it's better to come between morning and afternoon, because later the Never Summer Mountain Range lies in the shadows.

The Gore Range itself is not prominent from this viewpoint, because it is far away, lying just east of the winter sport city of Veil, 55 miles from here. It can be seen faintly in the distance, left of the impressive Never Summer Mountains. A clear view is needed to even notice the range. Anyway, the overlook is always worth a stop.

Longs Peak and Stones Peak

Part of the grand view from the Alpine Visitor Center into the glacial cirque.

(9) Alpine Visitor Center 11,796 ft

The Alpine Visitor Center is the highest visitor center in any national park. It is located at 11,796 feet at Fall River Pass. Besides the visitor center, where an exhibition tells you about life above the treeline, a gift shop with a cafeteria is ready to serve you. It takes care of visitors that got hungry or thirsty during a long day. It's the only place in the park where you can get food. During the winter months the visitor center, like Trail Ridge Road, is closed. It gets covered by snow, which insulates the building as an igloo does, keeping the temperatures at 20 degrees Fahrenheit or above. When the road opens on Memorial Day weekend, the park rangers usually need to dig the visitor center out of the snow masses covering it. All in all the Alpine Visitor Center is well worth a visit.

The Alpine Visitor Center is built at the edge of a glacial cirque. Take a peek behind the building and you will be surprised by an astonishing view into the bowl-shaped cirque. Different information boards will tell you, how the glacial cirque was created. At first

there were large amounts of snow, that — over millions of years — formed one glacier after another. Then these glaciers moved downhill, carving the bowl shape out of the mountainside, creating the glacial cirque. Looking down into the bowl you will see a beautiful scenery. To the left of the cirque Old Fall River Road is winding it's way up on the mountainsides of Mount Chapin and Marmot Point. This road was the original way to get to the Alpine Visitor Center, before Trail Ridge Road was built in 1932.

The Alpine Visitor Center

(10) Alpine Ridge Trail *11,796 - 12,005 ft*

Is it steep? Yes!

The Alpine Ridge Trail starts at the Alpine Visitor Center. It is short but steep — a 200 feet change in altitude over a quarter of a mile. Nowadays the trail is made of concrete with 220 stairs leading upwards. Not a big deal for moderately to well trained people and also usually not for children, since they don't carry much weight. But it's highly strenuous for the untrained, especially because of the altitude and the lack of oxygen. Take your time, if you want to explore it, but feel the thin air getting to you. Also the trail is open to all sides, making you vulnerable to the often strong winds — on most days it would be a good idea to bring a jacket along.

Next to the trail you will find plenty of wildflowers to enjoy — small plates will tell you which is which. You might even see the occasional marmot or pika. While you move uphill, give your lungs a chance to catch up on oxygen and turn around. The glacial cirque, at which the Alpine Visitor Center is built, surprises with many shades of yellow, brown, green and red, which match perfectly with the blue and white sky. Have a look around: you should notice more glacial cirques on the surrounding mountains.

Once you made it up the mountainside, the views from this 12,005 feet high peak are gorgeous. You are surrounded by rough alpine terrain and snow covered peaks — the Never Summer Mountains and the Mummy Range among others.

Overleaf: The Alpine Visitor Center is built at the edge of a glacial cirque

South view from the top of the Alpine Ridge Trail with Specimen Mountain to the right

Marmot Point (front left) seen from the Medicine Bow Curve Trail

(11) Medicine Bow Curve *11,660 ft*

From the Never Summer Mountain Range in the southwest up to Fairchild Mountain in the Mummy Range in the northeast, the Medicine Bow Curve gives you a wide angled view. Even though there is an information board that explains what you see, it is hard to distinguish the partly tiny and faint peaks, if you are not familiar with the mountains and ranges in this area. From an altitude of 11,660 feet, having clear weather, this curve offers you a grand view up to the Medicine Bow Mountains (20 mi) and into Wyoming (35 mi). The creek in the valley below is the Cache la Poudre River, that flows towards the plains in the east. The Medicine Bow Curve is a good place to turn around, if you don't want to drive the Trail Ridge Road all the way to the Kawuneeche Valley.

There is also a short, unofficial trail leading to the north. It is almost level and rewards you with beautiful views of the Mummy Mountains from their soft side. The weather-beaten Sundance Mountain is to the right of Marmot Point, while you can see Mount Chapin, Chiquita Mountain and Ypsilon Mountain just behind the left side of Marmot Point. Behind them you can catch a glimpse of Fairchild Mountain and Hagues Peak, both more than 13,500 feet high.

Medicine Bow Curve Trail

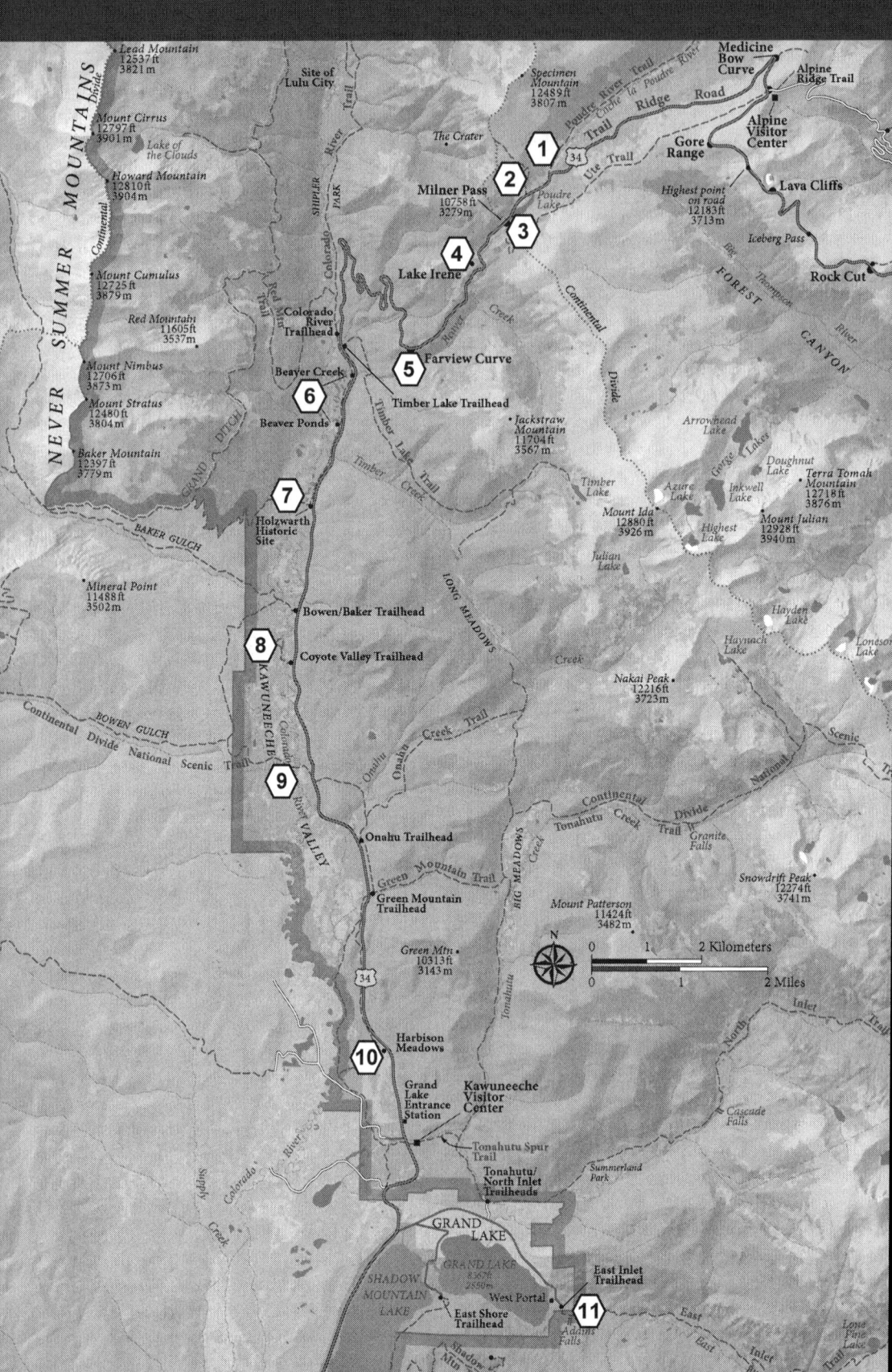

WEST TRAIL RIDGE ROAD

The western part of Trail Ridge Road, for the purposes of this book, starts after Medicine Bow Curve, the northernmost point of the road, and leads all the way down to the western park exit at Grand Lake. The views on this side of the park are dominated by the Kawuneeche Valley and the Never Summer Mountains, framing the valley. Trail Ridge Road quickly descends after Medicine Bow Curve below the treeline. The first three stops are located just before the Continental Divide near Poudre Lake. After passing the divide the stops become more disseminated and start focusing on the Kawuneeche Valley, the first being Farview Curve, offering an overview of the valley.

Kawuneeche means coyote in the language of the native Arapaho. The valley was created by glaciers and the same Colorado River that formed the Grand Canyon. Being close to its headwaters at La Poudre Pass on the northern park border, it winds its way as a rather small stream through the valley.

To watch moose, Kawuneeche Valley is the best place in the park. Even before dusk the majestic animals venture from the forest of the Never Summer Wilderness, to feed on the lush green of the swamplands. In spring, the cows are being accompanied by their calves. These are hard to spot in the high grass, protecting them from predators. A good starting point for your photo hunt of moose is the southern entrance to Bowen Trail, about a mile south of the Coyote Valley Trailhead.

① Cache la Poudre River *10,720 ft*

The Cache la Poudre River originates in the Poudre Lake, just across the street from the trailhead of the Poudre River Trail. The river starts tiny and small. It meanders through the beautiful Cache la Poudre Valley. An easy to walk but long trail leads you from the Poudre River Trailhead through the entire Cache la Poudre Valley. After 8.8 miles it meets the Corral Creek Trail just outside the northern border of the park. Peek into the trail and enjoy the wonderful meadows and the subalpine forest, but don't forget to turn around sometime, if you don't want to spend a night in the wilderness.

Birthplace of the Cache la Poudre River

The waters of the at first tiny river travel northeast and then north through the park and the contiguous Roosevelt National Forest. Later they turn east, where they formed the beautiful Poudre Canyon. At the northern edge of Fort Collins the river leaves the mountains and supplies the farms and communities of the eastern plains with water.

Cache la Poudre Valley

② The Crater   *11,480 ft*

The Crater Trailhead lies opposite from Poudre Lake at 10,740 feet, directly at Trail Ridge Road. Only a few parking lots are available here, but you can also park at Milner Pass and walk the few feet uphill to the trailhead. The hike to the Crater is steep and strenuous, 740 feet uphill, but only a mile long and well worth the effort. After about half the

Mule deer near Crater Trail

distance you reach the treeline and venture into the alpine tundra before reaching The Crater. You should be prepared for strong winds and a resulting wind-chill factor.

The Crater is a part of Specimen Mountain, whose summit lies to the right. The mountain was covered with volcanic material, when the Never Summer Mountains erupted. Erosion then exposed the volcanic remnants. Together with the crater-like shape this led to the wrong belief, that it were a volcanic crater, hence the name. If you get lucky you will be able to see some bighorn sheep, since a herd is living on the mountain. For their protection the Crater Trail is permanently closed from the overlook to the summit of Specimen Mountain. Also the entire trail is closed from May to July due to the lambing season of the bighorn sheep.

The trail was never officially built, but developed from more and more people using it. It was later supported by the park service, which built a parking lot at the trailhead. Due to instabilities and damage to the tundra, the trail was closed in 2014. Currently the park service is determining, whether it should be re-opened, relocated or permanently closed in order to protect sheep and tundra. We hope it stays open. It's a great opportunity to experience the transition from subalpine forest to tundra on a short trail.

The Crater with the Never Summer Mountains in the back

Poudre Lake at Milner Pass

⟨3⟩ Milner Pass *10,758 ft*

The parking lot at Milner Pass lies at the southern end of the beautiful Poudre Lake. It also gives access to the Ute Trail, which goes all the way across the tundra to Upper Beaver Meadows on the eastern side of the park or to the south to Farview Curve. Milner Pass is the point where Trail Ridge Road crosses the Continental Divide. The Continental Divide is a hydrological division, meaning every drop of water falling on the divide has to decide whether it wants to flow east or west. All streams starting east of the divide go to the Atlantic, all on the west go to the Pacific.

⟨4⟩ Lake Irene *10,698 ft*

Though parking is limited at Lake Irene, you should usually be able to squeeze in, because the visitation is also limited. Many people don't seem to know that they are missing out on a short and easy hike to a beautiful lake. Or you just park and use one of the tables for a picnic.

The round-trip to Lake Irene is less than a mile and starts out at 10,750 feet going downhill for just 50 feet. After crossing a wooden bridge you can soon spot the quiet lake. If it's dry, you can also have your picnic on the lush meadows surrounding the lake. The trail will lead you directly there if you stay to the right.

Lake Irene

⟨5⟩ Farview Curve   *10,120 ft*

View into the Kawuneeche Valley

Never Summer Mountains

Beaver Ponds

Beaver Creek Picnic Area

From this 10,120 feet high overlook you can see the Kawuneeche valley on the left side of the curve and the Never Summer Mountains on its right side. In between pine trees are blocking the sight.

The Never Summer Mountains are a volcanic range. While Longs Peak bestrides the east side of the park, much of the west side is dominated by the Never Summer Mountains. If you take a closer look at this range you will notice a horizontal cut along the mountains. This is the 14 miles long Grand Ditch, built between 1890 and 1932. It catches water from the mountains and conducts it to the eastern side of the Continental Divide. From there it feeds the Cache la Poudre River to supply the communities on the plains.

If you want to take a closer look at the ditch be prepared for a longer hike. From the Holzwarth Historic Site the Ditch Road goes directly up to the ditch. Farther north the Red Mountain Trail starting at the Colorado River Trailhead leads several miles in large switchbacks up the mountain before it follows the Grand Ditch Road. To the south the Baker Trail leads to the Ditch.

⟨6⟩ Beaver Creek & Ponds   *9,022/8,989 ft*

These two places are not trailheads, but picnic areas. Since they are on the less visited west side of the park, they are usually not crowded. Both picnic areas are very beautiful and rather quiet, even though they are close to the road. They provide a great view over the wetlands of the upper Kawuneeche Valley where the Colorado River is still just a little creek. One can truly say that the spirit of the Rocky Mountains can be felt at these places.

The Beaver Creek Picnic Area has four tables, Beaver Ponds six. Each table has its own fire grate, ready for you to get a barbecue going. At Beaver Ponds you can also use your own portable grill. But please pay attention to the fire warning level in the park. If there is a high danger of a wildfire, grilling will not be permitted.

⟨7⟩ Holzwarth Historic Site   *8,884 ft*

The "Mama" cabin

A pleasant half mile level walk, from the parking lot through the Kawuneeche Valley meadows, leads you to the Holzwarth Historic Site, which displays some of the park's rich history. When all hope for mining silver and gold in the Kawuneeche Valley vanished, the few people left in this region focused on mountain tourism. The Holzwarth family were German immigrants who built their ranch in 1918. When the Old Fall River Road was finished in 1920, the number of tourists increased dramatically. The Holzwarths turned their farm into the Holzwarth Trout Lodge, offering lodging, food and outdoor experiences. While the outbuildings of the complex that the family created are long gone, as well as the Never Summer Ranch to which they expanded their business, this historic site gives you a great insight into ranching and tourism in the early years of the park.

⟨8⟩ Coyote Valley Trail   *8,840 ft*

The Coyote Valley Trailhead is close to the road and hosts a picnic area as well as an accessible, one mile interpretive round-trip with several places to rest in between. Since coyote means kawuneeche in the local native language, the trail is a namesake to the valley. Coyotes are at home here as well as many birds like kingfishers and ospreys. The Coyote Valley Trail is a good place to experience life in a riparian habitat. Pause for a moment and listen to the steady, calming ripple of the Colorado River. Smell the pines, spruces and firs. Feel the soft wind and the warming sun on your cheeks.

Colorado River with Baker Mountain to the left

⑨ Moose Viewing *8,799 ft*

Moose are incredible creatures. They are tall and strong, yet they hide their beauty in the woods. Only during dusk and dawn will they come out to feed on the lush meadows and swamplands. While moose viewing is possible everywhere in the Kawuneeche Valley, we have been most successful finding them in the area close to the southern access point of the Bowen Trail. Not only wetlands but also protective spots with trees and bushes are nearby. Look out for moose in the wet meadows close to the street as well as all the way to the forest west of the Colorado River.

A moose stalking in Kawuneeche Valley

But remember to keep some distance for your safety. Especially cows with their offspring will be ready to defend themselves against intruders. Other areas where moose can be watched are the Coyote Valley Trail and the Harbison Meadow as well as Sprague Lake and Bear Lake on the east side of the park.

⑩ Harbison Meadows *8,704 ft*

For 30 years Annie and Kitty Harbison let their cows graze in this lush meadow to provide the town of Grand Lake with high quality milk. The house of the Harbisons has decayed long ago. But the sagebrush found in the meadow is still a witness of the grazing, which destroyed the grass, leaving room for sagebrush to grow. Since these sturdy plants can live 100 years and more, the reclaiming by grasses takes a long time. Today the Harbison Meadows are a nice and quiet picnic area where elk, moose, coyotes and other wildlife roam.

Sagebrush covers the Harbison Meadows

⑪ Adams Falls *8,460 ft*

The Adams Falls are accessible from the town of Grand Lake outside the park. The East Inlet Trailhead north of town, just at the border of the national park, is where the trail starts. From there the Adams Falls are just a short and easy hike of 0.3 miles away, gaining only 70 feet in altitude.

At the falls you first reach a viewing area, that lets you look down on the cascading falls. From there you can continue on the trail, following the Adams Falls for about 100 yards with several good views back towards the viewing area. At the end you can either turn around or continue to follow the trail. If you continue, it will also take you back to the trailhead on a loop totaling 0.9 miles.

Overleaf: An alpine thistle catches the last beams of the setting sun at Forest Canyon Overlook

Adams Falls in September

Printed in Great Britain
by Amazon.co.uk, Ltd.,
Marston Gate.